Kissing School

Kissing School

Seven Lessons on Love, Lips, and Life Force

Cherie Byrd

SASQUATCH BOOKS
SEATTLE

"Kiss My Dimple" (p. 32), reprinted with permission from Teri Anne Wilson and Suze Sims.

Printed in Canada
Published by Sasquatch Books
Distributed by Publishers Group West
14 13 12 11 10 09 08 07 06 05   6 5 4 3 2 1

Art direction: Kate Basart
Cover and interior illustrations: Kate Gebert
Book design and composition: Bill Quinby

Library of Congress Cataloging-in-Publication Data

Byrd, Cherie.
     Kissing school : Seven lessons on love, lips, and life force / Cherie Byrd.
        p. cm.
     ISBN 1-57061-440-7
     1. Kissing. I. Title.

     GT2640.B87 2005
     394—dc22   2004051032

Sasquatch Books / 119 South Main Street, Suite 400 / Seattle, WA 98104
(206) 467-4300 / www.sasquatchbooks.com / custserv@sasquatchbooks.com

I dedicate this book to Jainon Miles Collis, and to all courageous lovers of deep heart and wide spirit.

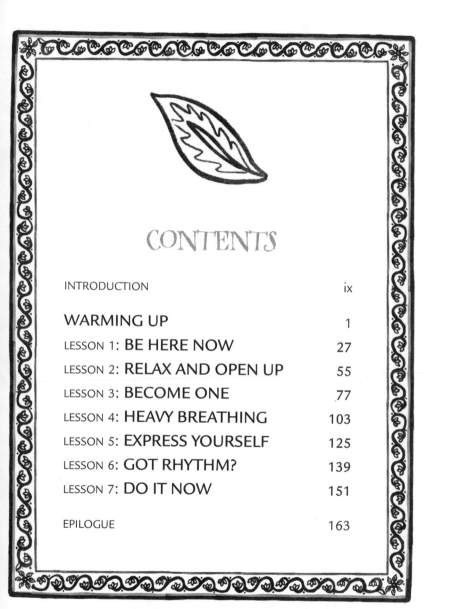

CONTENTS

Acknowledgments

I wish to thank all my students and clients who've courageously blossomed before my eyes, as well as the enlightened teachers who've shared their wit and wisdom so freely with me. Deep appreciation goes to Cyn Liggett, Kissing School's Goddessa of Operations, and to Joan Broughton, April Butcher, Sara Schurr, and Harmony for their generous support, insight, and assistance. Bless you all; you've been invaluable.

I have found men who didn't know how to kiss. I've always found time to teach them.

——*Mae West, 20th-century American entertainer*

Introduction

*f*lashback to 1997: I was dating a wonderful 57-year-old man who was a horrible kisser; clumsy, unskilled, and half-hearted. Yuck! How, I asked myself, does a person get to be this age and not know how to kiss? Then I pondered other men I'd dated over the years who were also clueless and wondered if this was a gender-specific dilemma. I began asking around and found out there were about as many women as men who were the cause of aborted relationships, because they didn't deliver in the kiss. It's a showstopper.

In the you-forever-after version of lovers, I also found lots of couples who'd stopped kissing a long time ago. I've been told it was too painful to continue repeating the badly delivered kiss; so they just tried to ignore it, hoping its loss wouldn't matter.

Most women I spoke with missed kissing greatly, that lusciousness of being deeply met with lip and tongue. They missed the surrender, the rapport, the playful heat. They missed how it made their body feel and they missed what it did to their hearts. Some of these women would not even let themselves feel their kissing hunger. To manage this containment they contracted their desires, their energy, their bodies, and their hearts so they could continue holding in their denial.

And the men? Some of the non-kissing men in these couples also shut down in denial, while others longed for the return of the red-hot kiss. Many of these guys confessed that they simply had no idea that they were missing out on some profound and joyful intimacy. If you don't know what you're missing, I guess it's not a problem—for you.

Kissing has always been one of my top three favorite activities. I know that I would shrivel up, shut down, and age mightily without this joyful celebration of merging. So, what to do? Here I am trying to connect with this new friend who is in the clueless category and therefore can't meet me in the dance of lip-loving. Do I pull away and move on, or do I do what I can to move closer? This is one of those tricky core questions I ask myself many times a day, not only in relationship to my partner, but in my relationship to life.

My deepest desires always urge me to go more fully, more openly into what life brings. But part of me is whining that I want someone different, someone who can already meet my standards, my desires. However, I really like this guy and do want to get to know him more deeply. Is the soulful, luscious, mouth-play of passionate kissing worth cultivating one more time? Yes. I want to see if we have what it takes to move into a deeper intimacy.

I told my unskilled boyfriend how much I missed luscious kissing, and that we would not survive a relationship unless he would let me teach him how to kiss. I figured I'd win either way. Miserable kisses leave me cold, hurt, frustrated, and more cranky than PMS. I was having no more, one way or another. He looked quizzical for a moment, sat up straight, then grinned and asked, "Does that mean we'll have a lot of homework?" You betcha!

Much to his surprise, kissing wasn't immediately on the menu. Teri Wilson, a songwriter friend of mine nailed it when she said, "There is more behind the kiss than meets the lips." It was necessary first to dig up and discard some old ideas and for some new groundwork to be laid.

I began with lessons on the energy dynamics of quantum physics so he could get an idea of what meeting and merging is essentially about. We did meditation practices to learn to be focused and get deeply present, explored ways of working with the body and its bioelectricity to engage its full potency, and practiced breathwork to enliven the charge within and between us. We brought all this into exploring the vibrant, sensual conversation of merging lips, expressive tongues, opening hearts, and pulsing bodies. No more lip-mashing, luv, there's a whole ocean of feelings and sensual conversing that wants to be shared. We were so very glad we'd both said yes.

Kissing School

Sitting at my computer a few weeks later I was typing up several class proposals for the local naturopathic college: Death and Dying, Human Sexuality, Perennial Philosophy, Energy Medicine. I teach from a multicultural, holistic frame, and I'd enjoyed these classes over the years. However, now there was a tiny voice calling from outside of my academic brain saying, "Noooo! I want to teach Kissing School!" Back inside the box of my brain, my inner academics rounded on this tiny voice saying, "You what?? That's appalling! You can't do that in public. All this education and you want to teach what?!" Scorn was heaped, but that radical new schoolteacher was grinning and wasn't giving up, not yet.

It didn't take a lot of researching on the Internet to find that nothing like what I had in mind existed; nor did it take many deep hours of pondering to realize that my heart would feel more successful teaching even one couple how to love each other fully and well than to teach a whole room of would-be physicians about Human Sexuality. Never mind teaching Death and Dying again; what people on their death-beds regret most is their lack of loving! Since any of us may die at any moment, learning to love more fully sounds like the most important, and most urgent, class to take. It also dawned on me that teaching kissing and pathways to deep intimacy would actually be fun! I get to cultivate a garden of loving energy. Wow. I know for certain that kissing needs to be taught somewhat playfully so its students can feel safe enough to open themselves to fresh juiciness. We actually learn more, and faster, if the process engages the body and is fun. Fun for students means fun for me! My choice was becoming clear. I didn't mail the university proposals, and the Inner Lovers offered the Inner Academics a seat in the back row of the peanut gallery.

The most healing and celebratory aspects of our lives are the loving moments we experience. I wonder where are the schools and teachers who model and encourage us to love, and love well from the depths of our being? In my research I've found that there are a couple of books printed on kissing. They make kissing into a game, an enter-tainment complete with silly names and ways to gross each other out. I have a different desire. I want to go deeper with students, explore and share what it takes to make a kiss an intimate, soulful, enlivening experience.

All my life I've felt compelled to participate in spiritual and heal-ing practices from many different schools of thought, both Western and Eastern, ancient and modern. I've also been involved in the arts in many forms and always somehow engaged in the creative process. And I've always *loved* kissing. I don't ever remember learning. Kissing seems like something I always knew, like I inherently knew how to sew as a child, or like I knew what people were feeling because I experienced (smelled, saw, and felt) their auras and how the energy flowed in their body. What I realized later in my studies is that my attention to art, energy reading, and spiritual practices actually trained me in the powers and practices basic to the ancient traditional sexual energy practices. I've found similar beliefs, intentions, and practices in Buddhist Tantra and Tibetan healing, Taoist sexual kung-fu, and western shamanic sexual arts.

These traditional arts of deep, energetically embodied, loving are part of my nature and became a part of my training. I wanted to distill the healing and spiritual values from the ancient systems, find their commonalities, and combine them with modern consciousness research for Kissing School. These are essential, foundational lessons for cultivating the energy and art of kissing, loving, and the experience of profound intimacy. These are also the same essential, foundational lessons for living a deep, empowered, healthy, and luscious life.

The Kissing School Book

Kissing School was opened in Seattle in 1998 and draws students internationally. It's time for the textbook, both for those who can and those who can't attend class. You'll find information and practices for adults of all ages and sexual orientations. This is a book for lovers who feel they missed out on their teenage lessons, as well as for those who feel they do have the basics. And these lessons are particularly vital for all of you who are technically good at kissing and now want to know how to cultivate the chemistry, the electricity, that is so powerfully moving.

Interest in Kissing School has come from all over the globe. Korea has had an abiding interest. TV interests in Korea call, leaving messages I can't unravel. A woman wants to include it in her Korean graduate studies. A young Korean student locally wants to write a paper on the topic. Just last week I was getting calls from the local Korean cable TV station, and my video flew off to Korea. Yesterday the Koreans arrived at my office with cameras, did interviews, and told me that Valentine's is *very* big in Korea. The Spanish community also wants to videotape me for one of their TV stations, and they have held interviews for their radio stations. They were very disappointed that my Spanish was rusty. *Lo siento.*

The Internet has done its share of activating worldwide interest; many students have found me there. The articles from local and national papers have also found their way around the globe. I've done radio interviews for New Zealand and two PBS stations in Australia. Switzerland, Thailand, and Peru have also requested interviews. In London the BBC got interviews. I've done radio interviews all over the United States, and since Kissing School was on Seattle TV last November it seems Seattle radio has finally gotten the news.

Students have come from all over Canada and the United States, and there are lists of groups that are forming for classes around the country. I also get requests for private groups that are interested in personal growth, including the Young Presidents' Organization. They'd all love a text—something that has some real meat to it, is meant for grown-ups, and yet is playful, rich, and relatively non-threatening . . . like the class.

So here I offer you the seven lessons I teach in my classes. You'll be learning how to cultivate and actualize your Inner Lover, discovering the depths of your inner resources and how to bring them into your intimate life. As you work your way through the Kissing School book, you'll find that there are several extra elements flowing through the text. All of the quotes, sidebars, and exercises are useful for taking you more deeply into the teachings. One of the reasons we stay stuck in any habit of mediocrity is that we have no imaginative imprint that calls us forward. These elements activate the imagination, stir the senses, and cultivate the qualities and the arts of the skillful lover.

Exercises are found in every chapter and are pathways for embodying the teachings and taking you directly into the experience of loving. Many of these exercises are meant for you alone. It is essential to have something to offer your beloved, and that something is you; so many of these practices are created to assist you in your own ability to love and to share that love skillfully. You may find yourself enjoying some exercises more than others. This may be because you're already good at the ones you enjoy. Real learning goes deeper when we stretch into something new; therefore, don't be timid, give yourself permission to experiment and grow. Share the lessons with your beloved. Read them to each other. Be playful, get past blame, fear, and ruts together. Talk about it at breakfast, practice a couple of exercises during your day, and explore the results in your evenings together.

The lessons and exercises of Kissing School build on each other, so the most potent practice would be to learn them in order. Because of the way our internal sexual energy system is wired, there are basic exercises in grounding and cultivating presence that bring more depth and fire into your system and truly empower the later lessons. There is no harm, however, in jumping into any area of the book that is calling you more deeply into loving. When you're ready, go back and catch what you may need for the full effect. You may find that keeping a journal of your experience with these exercises helps you to further ground and deepen your practice in the love zone. Perhaps you and your beloved will write in the same journal, sharing the pillow talk, writing love notes, being grateful for a lover who is willing to grow with you.

And so, dear lovers, I invite you to read on and enter the world of passionate kisses.

WARMING UP

It is the passion that is in a kiss that gives to it its sweetness; it is the affection in a kiss that sanctifies it.

—*Christian Nestell Bovee, 19th-century American writer*

A Peck Is Just a Peck

I paused on my way from the teapot to the computer to watch a few minutes of the early morning TV news. It was just before Valentine's Day, so the program was featuring a dozen newly married couples celebrating their weddings. I was astonished to see over and over again that the only kisses taking place on this, the most romantic occasion of their lives, were little smacks—hard, fast pecks. *Bang! Bump! Smack! Bounce!*

It felt like such a missed opportunity. What was going on? Were the bride and groom too stressed out at that point to even make contact with each other? Were they in such a mad rush to get past the celebrating, and on to the wedding bed, that they couldn't have taken ten more seconds to actually kiss? Wasn't this celebration supposed to be the golden moment for loving and kissing—communing with their beloved's heart, maybe melting into each other a bit, taking a deep breath and swooning? Where was the love, the being intimately seen and celebrated? I saw no signs of anyone sharing deep feelings during any of these weddings, and frankly, that scared and saddened me. Are we really so out of touch with our hearts?

Why is it that so many of the kisses we experience are less than bell-ringing? From my experience teaching Kissing School, I've discovered that 90 percent of the kisses people share are little more than pecks on the fly. Is a peck really a kiss, or is it a substitute for a kiss?

A peck more often sends a passive-aggressive message: "I don't really wanna feel anything here, but I'm supposed to kiss you, so here, take this dead, duty-bound, discounting gesture and be glad for it, because I have other, more important things to attend to." *Smack! Buzz!*

Peck! Peck! Peck! No loving is delivered, no savoring of the moment or relishing of each other. You've missed each other, and this repeated sense of loss unwittingly builds walls of hurt, resentment, numbness, and isolation.

At best, a peck is a split-second token of affection between the surfaces of two egos with different agendas. You're left wanting and empty. The lover is hungry for a juicy morsel and is given a few grains of sand to chew. *Blech!* Relationship starvation. Where's the feast? Where are those essential nutrients of loving energy that you hunger to have rushing through your body, melting your heart, touching your soul?

If any "loving" expression is more ineffective than the peck, it's got to be the pat-pat-pat on the back that frequently goes with the peck. The pat-pat-pat has even been known to put the "discount and dismissal" cap on what could have been a fairly good kiss. Why treat your beloved like a distant relative, or like your pet? Even your dog would rather have a good rub, or a little fondling of the ears, than a smack-smack-smack on the back. This kind of pseudo-hug is another duty contact, and it feels not loving or comforting, but condescending and dismissive.

Being enfolded into someone's vulnerable, soft, warm body, merging right through their skin into their deepest self, is one of the most healing and heartwarming of experiences. Why would we want to miss out on the opportunity to reach out and embrace the ones we love?

Am I saying that pecking and patting are *never* more than tokens of duty and dismissal? Actually, yes: the energy of duty and dismissal is built into the nature of the peck-pat. That's not to say all kisses have to be long, drawn-out encounters, however. Sometimes a heartful tiny kiss or a sensitive small touch can be the most comforting of gestures, depending on the quality of presence that is being offered with it.

You can gaze into someone's eyes, even those of a friend or a relative, and, finding their sorrow, give them a tiny sweet kiss of comfort. Hearts can melt, feelings flow. In that small fraction of time, the depth of life is tasted. Although sorrow is bitter, it becomes bittersweet when shared with genuine affection. This is an open and spontaneous expression of your heart and may be the perfect gift for an intimate moment.

At times, a hand lightly placed on your arm or your back is the exact balm you need. Why is it that some touch has the power to melt your walls of pain and stress and can pull you directly and fully into this moment? What makes this sweet and loving gesture so different from the buzz-peck-pat-you-ma'am that feels so empty and dismissive? Why are some kisses, some caresses, luscious and divine, and others frustrating, painful experiences?

There is the kiss of welcome and of parting; the long, lingering, loving, present one; the stolen, or the mutual one; the kiss of love, of joy, and of sorrow; the seal of promise and receipt of fulfillment.

——*Thomas C. Haliburton, 19th-century Canadian writer*

Kissing Lessons

I wonder, have people locked the doors to their inner selves because they give themselves no time to live and love from there? Or is it really that they've never cultivated the necessary skills for hearing and sharing their depths? Either way they continue to miss out, living life with only their surfaces meeting.

What are the elements of a meaningful and luscious kiss? How do we physically and energetically share the gifts of our deepest selves? What does it take to cultivate a rich intimacy between two people, and how do we unintentionally block it? You may be surprised to find that it's less about mechanics than about the quality of attention and energy that informs our actions: a thrilling touch, a sumptuous kiss, a coy glance.

What does it take to be able to transmit and receive subtle, rich, flowing signals of connection, heat, and heart? The first step is to recognize that you really do want a more fulfilling, loving relationship. You're hungry, and the love substitutes are not filling the deeper ache.

The second step is to make an intentional decision to do what it takes to create deep and growing intimacy. Many of us need to begin with some lessons on getting out of our heads and cultivating a fully embodied presence in order to experience our lives directly, in our bodies. It may involve learning to open your heart and bringing this open-heartedness into the midst of your living. It almost always means cultivating a deep sensitivity and awareness of your own experience, as well as what your beloved is experiencing.

Ultimately, intimacy is about being vulnerable to life, to the fullness of this moment, and to the sweet essence of your spirit. This allows you to develop empathy for those vulnerable depths in your loved ones. Intimacy is felt, your soul is touched, sweetness flows into loving—embodying, enlivening, and heating your actions. You're in the love zone, and feasting happens here. You come away from this sublime kiss feeling tasted, delighted upon, devoured. And in offering your tender, open-hearted kiss, you also receive all that luscious energy, and so you become sated and sassy.

Is it really possible to bring all this flowing passion and intimacy into a kiss? Yes! The *kiss sublime* is a fabulous vehicle for cultivating love and sharing your most precious gifts. It's what kisses are for!

Making Contact

There are days and weeks when we give too little of ourselves and are left feeling disconnected from the important people in our lives. Silent contact with a loved one, intentionally shared, can begin to rebuild your rapport.

Try nuzzling foreheads with your sweetie or kids or sister. Caress their cheeks with your hands and draw their forehead to yours. Breathe deeply. Close your eyes and take a moment to really cherish them. You can actually give and receive a lot of communication and affection from this small gesture.

Women still remember the first kiss after men have forgotten the last.

—*Remy de Gourmont, 19th-century French writer and philosopher*

Every Impression Is a first Impression

The first kiss in any relationship is a pivotal experience, and one that may set the stage for the rest of the relationship. We anticipate and wait for it. We long for it. We look forward to melting in its glow. We know when it happens. What are we expecting? Why, the perfect kiss, the one we've always wanted, the kiss that will awaken all the forces of love within us, the one that we hope is just about to arrive.

So often we miss that target. There's nothing more discouraging to a budding relationship than anticipating the succulent communion of that first kiss but receiving a heartless peck or a mushy, slobbery lip-mash instead. What happened to the promise of connection, warmth, and feeling?

Whether this heartless, unskilled gesture happens on the first date or in the twentieth year of marriage, it's a shock. We close down in response, because we're hurt to be so unmet. Since we can assume that was not our partner's intent, we may find that a wounded or uneducated Inner Lover lives within him or her. Sadly, wounds beget more wounds, since we respond to hurt by slamming the gates of own hearts with our held breath and tense body, defending ourselves from another assault of heartless lips.

We can only learn to love by loving.

—*Iris Murdoch, British writer*

Inner Lovers

Deep and luscious loving is the cherished art form of your *Inner Lover*. Who is your Inner Lover? Your Inner Lover dwells in the deepest part of your heart and knows what love feels like. It's the part of you that longs for the warmth of genuine acceptance and the spacious freedom of an unconditional embrace.

Inner Lovers bridge the romantic nature of your emotional body with the depth of love that arises from your spirit. Inner Lovers yearn to cultivate a life of deep loving that reveals the resonance of the deepest Self in your body. This deep connection unites a Self that feels secure, supported, and free with a loving heart that is warm, vulnerable, soft, and intensely potent. This is communion experienced directly in your body, one that is sensually and energetically connected to your life.

In this time of information overload, lifestyle coaches, and personal trainers, I find almost no one who believes that we ourselves can educate these abandoned and clueless Inner Lovers to become deep, intimate, potent, and fulfilled. Too few of us are aware that loving and sexual energy can regenerate and heal us, offering a luscious counterpoint to the wear and intensity of our lives.

The Department of Tenderness

"People don't cuddle anymore, and that's the reason why there are so many conflicts," Antoine Denert, mayor of the Belgian town of Kruibeke, declared one day in 2003. Denert's solution? He set up a Department of Tenderness to encourage people to be nicer to each other—and assumed the top spot himself. "I will set an example," he explained, "and start in my own village by caressing, cuddling and kissing as many people as possible." Denert has said he hopes national and international institutes will follow his example. Wouldn't that be astounding?

sub·li·mate

To modify the natural expression of a primitive, instinctual impulse in a socially acceptable manner.

To divert the energy associated with an unacceptable impulse or drive into a personally and socially acceptable activity.

——American Heritage Dictionary

To Sublimate or Not to Sublimate

In our modern culture, we've split ourselves off from the impulses and energies of our body, our emotions, and our spiritual resources in order to function primarily from the intellect in an extremely mental world. This split blocks three-fourths of our direct experiences and diverts or sublimates them into a mentalized perception. Life becomes hard, and driven.

Why would we sublimate the wild lusciousness of our instinctual loving to achieve the safety of a "socially acceptable activity"? Cultural training, mostly. For centuries, most "civilized" people have been taught to fear the potency of passion, the power of love, and the expression of an unguarded heart. The same can be said for our direct experience of our spirit. How many thousands of years have we been taught to seek the wisdom and power of our spirit through the medium of others? And so we've learned to control, manage, and contain our impulses, thinking that we are keeping ourselves safe. Safe from unexpected love? Safe from freedom of expression? Safe from feeling too alive?

This reined-in loving and living is a practice of protection, not intimacy, and is based on the idea that our natural impulses are not to be trusted. With these guarded moments we build walls between ourselves and our partners, and between ourselves and life's vital forces. Our body builds a dam of locked tension between our heads and bodies. Our breathing and our loving become shallow.

For this sublimation of our body's experience, we pay a high price. Our body is designed to be *an amplifier of our inner experience,* to enrich us with the felt qualities of our lives. When we choose not to engage this natural embodied awareness in our moment-to-moment consciousness, we lose touch with our inner self. We become dispirited, numb, and disconnected; we feel out of touch with ourselves and what we are experiencing. When sublimation defines the edges of our loving, we develop habits of bodily closure, we settle for less and less as the walls of defense thicken, and we're left as isolated, bored, and unfulfilled lovers.

You Kissed Me

You kissed me! My head drooped low on your breast
With a feeling of shelter and infinite rest,
While the holy emotions my tongue dared not speak,
Flashed up as in flame, from my heart to my cheek;
Your arms held me fast; oh! your arms were so bold—
Heart beat against heart in their passionate fold.
Your glances seemed drawing my soul through mine eyes,
As the sun draws the mist from the sea to the skies.
Your lips clung to mine till I prayed in my bliss
They might never unclasp from the rapturous kiss.

—Josephine Slocum Hunt, 19th-century British poet

Hungry for Deep Love

We rarely share the depths of our love, so for much of life we are actually training each other *not* to feel the radiance and freedom of loving energy. We're practicing being less than our fullness. We are also practicing receiving less than fullness, and generating reciprocal inadequacy, so both we and our partners feel inadequately loved. What we practice regularly is what becomes our habit, and in this case we're practicing mediocre loving and are left wanting.

Bodies, hearts, and souls hunger for true intimacy in these stressful times. Our lives are full of busyness, and our Inner Lovers have been relegated to dark closets, forgotten and unfed. These repeated messages of habitual closure and *love hunger* are stored in our cellular memory and are ultimately what make us sick and tired. You may find your Inner Lover feeling ignored, closed off, and desperately hungry.

Your disconnect is readily conveyed through your kiss, your touch, your heartless distraction, so you find your dilemma of sublimation arising even in your attempts to connect. Unmet lovers feel cheated. They come to believe that intimacy, sex, and even kisses don't live up to the promises, the fantasy.

Role models openly practicing sublime loving are precious and rare. But without role models, how can we learn to relax, open, and cultivate our Inner Lovers? Without role models, most of us just don't know how to bridge the gap between the mediocrity of what is and the dream of what we deeply want. Few lovers know the price they pay for sublimating, or how potent and life-enhancing the energy of their heart truly is. We often have little or no experience feeling, or even observing, the power of unsublimated loving and haven't dreamed that *sooo* much more is available in this flamboyant dance of love, lip, and life force. Can we go beyond the fantasy and discover something deeply real that springs from the core of who we truly are? Clearly, we need a new vision.

Allow desire to draw you into the deepest giving of love possible. When you yearn for your lover, don't resist the desire, but also don't attach it to something less than your deepest feeling-truth. No carnal embrace in itself equals eternal love. No anatomical perfection satisfies the emptiness of gifts ungiven. No genital friction adds up to the fire of the heart unbound.

—David Deida, American writer

Tapping Your Source

It's much too easy to spin in tight, protective, defensive positions that close your heart and ultimately cut you off from your own warm, loving self, as well as from those around you. To reclaim your heart means to reclaim *all* that your heart has experienced and all it desires. It is important to learn heart-opening practices that embrace without sublimation the full range of who you are: your pain and your passion, your disillusionment and your deepest knowing. In this embrace of your whole self you extend internal grace and acceptance to yourself and begin to bring yourself back into your own heart, body, and soul. This is an intimate chat with your Inner Lover and is the primary necessity before you can share your loving self.

Opening Your Heart

Lore in almost every traditional culture, East and West, tells us that the source of our Being, the deepest core of humanity, lives in our hearts. Sometimes the teachings are speaking of the soul, sometimes the spirit, sometimes the ties that bind one human to another. Whether we know of these ancient tales or not, it's clear to any feeling person that a closed heart offers small, cold comfort. Simple practices for opening the heart can begin to melt the icy walls of separation and cultivate a sweet, warm invitation to intimacy.

1. Find a few moments for silence, alone, preferably in a beautiful place. Sit comfortably and close your eyes. Bring your attention to your breath, and begin to drop some of the tension in your body as your breath deepens.

2. Breathe deeply: Begin your breath in your belly area and open a large inhalation, traveling up into your upper chest. Exhale back down into your belly. Follow this with your mind and internal senses for six breaths.

3. Now, when your inhaling breath comes up into your breast area, imagine a bright light igniting itself inside the center of your chest. Let this light expand outside your skin for several inches. You may see it, or imagine it, but certainly *feel it.*

4. When you exhale, allow the light to flood through you, out into the world. Continue for ten or more breaths. Stay present; keep feeling everything.

5. Continue feeling this open-hearted presence as your day unfolds.

This exercise allows you to open your heart chakra, the energy center in the middle of the chest (more on this in Lesson 4), and let out some love. Can you feel the sweetness, the paradoxical safety in this openness? This is you peeking out!

Pure vulnerability is the truest aphrodisiac.

—Anonymous

Old Lessons on Love, Lips, and Life force

A ncient cultures have often had explicit teachings on love and loving, many of which survive today. In many cultures sexuality and loving were intimately woven into medical teachings and recognized as potent healing energies. Sexual potency was a measure of radiant health, and one was expected to cultivate sexual life force right up to death.

The puritanical American culture that many of us grew up in is clearly not offering these teachings, even if it is pointing out organ names and functions in grade school. Many of us have learned about kissing and loving from families who shared more dysfunctional anguish than passion, and who had marginal relational skills. Where are the schools that model and encourage us to love, and love well from the depths of our being?

Our culture is missing out on something essential that many traditional ancient cultures knew about and held in high regard. They knew what kind of energetic, open-hearted presence it takes to be a potent and healing lover, and how to cultivate this energy. They had an embodied, sensual rapport with life force that we seem to have lost.

All through recorded history, there have been schools for the loving arts where men and women were trained in the arts of giving and receiving love. These schools had various intentions: healing the war out of returning soldiers, cultivating life force and physical vitality, achieving heightened states of spiritual union, or enhancing the realms of intimacy in daily life. They've left us a rich, if little-known, legacy for tapping into the sublime.

Teachings on the cultivation and use of sexual energy are as old as the hills. At the core of traditional shamanic practices is a body of spiritualized sexual energy practices and longevity wisdom that takes both shaman and student deeply into the vibrational frequencies of love. Shamans evolve to become those rare, realized, luminous beings who embody truth and love in their very existence, who are a model of what is possible. The Toltec of Mexico, a currently expanding community known as the keepers of the wisdom, teach practices for mastery of sexual energy in combination with practices for healing and cultivating enlightened awareness. These teachings are traditionally available to everyone, with the shamans taking the lessons even deeper to cultivate the necessary quantum of energy for their healing and visionary gifts.

The Hindu and Buddhist tantric sacred sexuality practices, as well as those of the Chinese Taoists, the Cherokee Quodoshka, and the Polynesian Huna, have much in common with these ancient cultivars of love. They acknowledge sexual energy as a carrier of the life force that, when combined with the power of the heart, inspirits and regenerates our lives.

In my journeys I have found that all Native people possess this core awareness [teachings of the shaman] at some level, or retain a piece of it. The remnants are as far-reaching as Siberia, Australia, the African continent, India, old civilizations of the Goddess, Asia, Polynesia, the Middle East and the Native Americas. . . . I have found that, in addition to the Toltec, the Nahuatl and the Maya, many other indigenous cultures have had the Nagual, or the Shapeshifter Sun and may have had knowledge of the Fire Within. The Q'ero, descendants of the Inka, are one such example. The Yaqui, Yuma and Dineh, as well as early Mississippian cultures, are yet others. Nagualism has been found to have its roots in the same knowledge pool that fed the pre-Tibetan and Siberian shamanic traditions, and these began long before, and occurred during, the trans-continental shamanic sweep, perhaps 40,000 years ago.

—*Merilyn Tunneshende, American writer and Toltec shaman*

Is there still more in store for me when, yielding to the profound feelings which overwhelm me, I draw from your lips, from your heart, a love which consumes me with fire?

—*Napoleon Bonaparte, 18th-century French emperor*

Paths to the Sublime

ractices for energy mastery, cultivation of a full-bodied presence, conscious sensuality, and life force enhancement are at the core of most traditional teachings. The life force factor in particular is vital for those wanting to experience passion. We all hear stories of depleted energy, hormones bottoming out, nonresponsive partners, marginalized interest, and general feelings of disconnect from the body. Developing resonant states of awareness within the bodily tissues is key. This means learning to move energy and empower the flow of communication between the body, emotions, mind and spirit. These are essential practices for an empowered life and empowered love.

When you are open and present in the body, sensual awareness can be deepened into a fine art. Subtle nuances become large events. The dance of emotional, physical, and spiritual energy within moves you, igniting the flames of your heart and spirit and loins, curling your toes.

The best kisses are inherently a spiritual experience because it is in these moments that we drop the walls between You and Me, and We merge. This act of moving beyond the experience of separation into resonant states of communion is both the definition of intimacy and the essence of mystical consciousness. It's a bonding of masculine presence and feminine life force (regardless of gender) in which there is a right-now rush of deep connection, naturally triggering a play of energies between you and your partner. When bodies are open to this flow, they vibrate synapses into hormonal flows that surge with life force, and we call that energy "chemistry." We experience a presence larger than the two sets of lips and skin, a presence that is our birthright and that is truly sublime.

sub·lime

Of high spiritual, moral, or intellectual worth.

Not to be excelled; supreme. Inspiring awe; impressive.

———*American Heritage Dictionary*

The Kiss Sublime

The not-to-be-excelled *kiss sublime* is a vehicle of intimacy: of hearts met and shared, warmth that becomes heat, resonance that becomes electricity. Intimacy that is all-encompassing and time-suspending simply lifts you into the sublime. In open sharing without boundaries, the Inner Lover moves out of frigid isolation and connects with the heat of inevitable bliss.

Sublime loving is a merging with your beloved and with the world around you, and it deeply affects your experience of yourself. You will find that its potent communion calls you to the creative edges of your life—to heights and depths of untapped heart, body, mind, and spirit. The wellsprings of love and awe are found in these wild frontiers of your inner landscape. It is here that you may rest safely in your open surrender, discover the love that is your deepest self, and cultivate the fine arts of sharing love supreme.

Developing a life in which loving in the body is a practiced art form offers you an opportunity to expand beyond disheartened isolation into a fully connected and embodied state of being. Real intimacy opens you and your beloved to the undistorted richness of the moment. The arts of the heart are practices that re-engage inherent warmth, that expand presence and the ability to share, allowing Inner Lovers to connect deeply with each other in the midst of living life.

What is necessary to regenerate the life force and to nourish your Inner Lover so that you can experience the chemistry of your own juice, heat, electricity, and healing? What does it take to allow love to fill you, overflowing into your kisses, your intimacy, your family, and your life? Mostly it takes education and practice. But it also takes a lot of internal permission, a gnawing hunger for a life of loving deeply, and an unwillingness to settle for anything less.

Lessons may be necessary, but remember that loving is essentially an art form and that your practice will largely be shaped by your willingness to be creative with what you are experiencing. Learning begins with being fully in the Now and claiming the rights of your unsublimated desires. Consider each desire an urgent invitation to bare your heart, to drop the walls between you and your partner. For what you really want to get is also what you really want to give—love, boundless love.

There is so much untapped potential: the naked promise in a glance, the electricity in a touch, the delicious merging of a kiss. A simple kiss, or even a touch, can eventually evolve into a fully orgasmic experience. It becomes possible not only to experience a full-body orgasm while loving but also to *be* a body-mind-heart-spirit that is orgasmically tuned.

In this fully connected state, one can experience from the slightest gesture the full rush of deep electrical surrender that we call orgasm: from a dance of lips, from a tongue sliding between your fingers, from a drop of water running down your spine. In fact, any point of connection with a partner, oneself, or the world, or even the mere *feeling* of communion, can melt our walls and swoon us open to love's rush and radiance.

And so I offer the following lessons to teach you to become artful, skilled, fully connected beings with awakened Inner Lovers. Educated Inner Lovers have the genuine ability to open deeply into loving, healing, and the warm presence of their inherently bright spirits. And so let's begin with the first of seven lessons and learn how to say *yes* to loving.

LESSON 1

Be Here Now

The loving are the daring.

—*Bayard Taylor, 19th-century American writer and traveler*

To Be Here or Not to Be Here

I t is the quality of your presence that is the measure of your intimacy. "Showing up" is the first step in creating anything of value. Being fully present, grounded in your body's experience, and open in this moment are essential skills for artful loving.

Over the last several decades I've studied innumerable techniques for cultivating personal power in all its forms: mental mastery, emotional expression and communication, physical re-creation, spiritual disciplines, and worldly manifestation. Whether these techniques were ancient teachings or modern technologies of empowerment, they all began with the need to potently, fully, show up in the present moment. So, following in the footsteps of the best of teachers, we can begin cultivating the intimacy of the *kiss sublime* by attending to just how we show up.

Countless books describe the intriguing ways our mouths and tongues can move around any piece of anatomy. These guidebooks assure us that if we master the buzzing of lips, the nibbling with teeth, the rubbing of skin, and the blowing into ears, we surely will get the love we're wanting. The promise is that we can be great lovers and experience deep and satisfying intimacy by mastering the mechanics of flirting, kissing, sexing, talking dirty, making up stories, and playing with toys. *Au contraire!* Nothing is more likely to generate empty, boring, going-through-the-motions attempts at intimacy than a mechanistic, technical approach.

This viewpoint is a strategic approach to loving that comes out of our culture's willful approach to living. You decide that you must **do** something specific to make a particular outcome happen, in order to *have* the something that will determine that you can *be* who you want to be. If you *do* what you must, you can *have* what you want, and therefore *be* the success you want to be. ***Do, have, be.***

Doing Intimacy

In the practice of loving, many people, especially those with a predominantly masculine sexual energy (as discussed later in this chapter), have embraced this strategic loving style. They're *doing* their partner. What you must *do* in this case is turn someone on. Do something to them, do lots of things, work it; get that fire going. Twiddle them this way and that, in the proper order, so you can *have* the outcome you desire, and *be* satisfied. Mission accomplished; game over.

Or perhaps you've invested your power in your partner; they're responsible for the heat. What you *do* then is get them to *do* the work of titillation; they need to turn you on in order for you to experience love. Something must be done, and done a certain way so that something else can be done, so you can go on to something else that is even better, and you're greedy for satisfaction so you want to hurry through all of this so you can get to the end where you can *have* the possibility of a fleeting moment of intimacy and then *be* a happy, fulfilled, satisfied person, at least for a brief time. You make something happen, to get the loving in order to be happy. Mission accomplished; game over. But love is not a goal to be finished with, dear hearts.

With a kiss let us set out for an unknown world.

—Alfred de Musset, 19th-century French poet and dramatist

Being Artful Lovers

K nowing the right musical notes and proper breathing techniques is essential for you to successfully sing a song; but a dry, tight, technically rendered melody will leave the audience hungry for some emotion, some soul. They want some *Inner You* inviting the *Inner Them* into a shared experience.

Colored paint put on a canvas is not art unless it's fed by an inner vision. Similarly, the intensity of your emotional heat, the power of your vision, and the juice of your inspiration nurture the shape, texture, and vibrancy of what arrives on the canvas of your life.

Intimate loving is a fine art, and as with any art it's certainly useful to have a repertoire of skills for the expression of your creative desires. Learn how talented your tongue really is, for instance. There are a bazillion nerve endings on the tip of your tongue that connect down into some highly sensitive areas below the belt. But before **doing** your beloved with those skills, go within yourself and call up your Inner Lover. That is who gets real heat going. Remember that Inner Lovers bridge the romantic natures of your emotional body with the abiding love that arises from your spirit. This is where passion is created; the inner connection of heart and soul ignites our body's experience of love. We **be** in touch with our love, and it is this that is shared with lip, tongue, and breath.

Sharing the feast of your essential **be**-ing through the vehicle of your artful skills, you will **have** the experience of loving, intimately.

Loving is a natural outcome of being fully Here and openly sharing this deep, radiant presence. There is an "intimacy zone" just as there is a sweet zone in any art or sport. To enter the intimacy zone, it is essential to be fully Here, Now.

The arts of managing lips, love, and life force are fueled by your Inner Lover's desires to be fully expressed and fully met. For this, your senses and attention need literally an attention that is finely connected to the senses. The quality of your attention determines how deeply met you will feel, and how many goose bumps you will create.

Kiss My Dimple

In the body's energy system, sexual energy and creativity are found together, nurturing each other. People who are artists of intimacy are also often free with their expressions and their creativity. You may paint more passion into your landscapes; or, like a couple of friends of mine, you may compose some saucy lyrics, wrap them in a world-beat tune, and perform them for my dancing delight!

Kiss my dimple
Kiss my dimple
Kiss it!
You're in a hurry, but what am I—
Some kind of slice of homemade pie?
Every part is edible that satisfies
I've flown and sewn around this world tonight
And you're simply thrilling me
But what I want to see is you
Kiss me on my dimple baby
But never let me go
It's evident by your urgency
There's no diffidence in emergencies
Well, you really had me going
We'll spoon ourselves to sleep
Learn that love is the key to life Now
Your love is lifting me straight through my heart
Kiss my dimple
Kiss my dimple

—Teri Anne Wilson and Suze Sims, 2002

My "first" kiss, I actually asked her permission. She sighed, as in res-
ignation, and then with some impatience she closed her eyes, puck-
ered her lips and then opened them only long enough to say, "Okay,
but make it quick," whereupon we engaged in the briefest and driest
moment in all erotica.

—*Phil Donahue, American talk-show host*

Hungry Ghosts

When kisses deliver no emotion, no resonance, no presence,
you're left wanting—maybe subtly, maybe deeply. When
there is a flatness to your beloved's gaze and a vacancy in
their response, you get hurt in a profound way; you have a sense of
being entirely missed. You're left hungry for the connection that did
not happen, for that flow of shared energetic juice. You didn't share
and didn't receive those life-giving nutrients, "Vitamin M" and "Vitamin F," *masculine* and *feminine sexual energy*. When your encounters lack
intimacy, you become nutrient starved, and your experiences leave you
haunted by nagging, hungry ghosts.

Hungry lovers often sublimate their primary longing for love and
look elsewhere in life for something that promises to fill the inner void.
Almost everything has been tried: eating chocolate, endless money
chasing, buying more stuff, smoking, and the pseudo-spirit found in
bottles. Hungry lovers are looking for something they cannot resist, to
which they can surrender themselves fully and thereby experience fullness. But they are not easily fooled: even if they do not know the full
depth of satisfaction possible in luscious, genuine loving, they recognize the emptiness of artificial love substitutes.

Deep, resonant intimacy comes from a genuine, Here-and-Now sharing of embodied energy—sensual, heartful stuff. Surrendering to this juicy, warm, sweet nourishment can break you free from the chaos on the surface of life, and pull you closer and closer to the strong, open love zone of your essential Self. As we open up, we develop the opportunity to become intimate with life everywhere, as vulnerable, open, feeling beings. **Be** an embodied, present lover, **do** artful sharing of your heart and soul, and you'll naturally **have** intimacy. Instead of the **do, have, be** routine, adopt a **be, do, have** approach: engage your inner self first. It all begins with being who you fully are.

Alchemy of Love

Try adding the elements of open-hearted enjoyment to any act of sublimation, and you'll come closer to feeding your deeper hunger. Practice, for example, with a piece of chocolate. Bring your excitement to the chocolate; yearn for it for a while before eating it. Inhale deeply its rich brown complexity. Let the aromas rush through your body. Salivate, and let your mouth come alive with full attention. Place a small piece in your mouth, and let your whole mouth feel and taste as your tongue caresses its melting smoothness against your palate. Breathe luxuriously and open your heart as you savor the fullness of this moment. *Mmmmm!*

Being Here Now with Someone Not Here Now

You can be close to those you love many times a day. No matter where they are on the globe, or even if they are no longer living, you can bring their presence energetically into your life Now.

1. Get fully present within yourself first. Stretch or shake your body to wake up inside your skin, while breathing deeply.

2. Sit down and imagine that your loved one is near you, sitting in front of you or resting in your arms, right Now. Feel their presence right into your body.

3. Connect with your own heart, and feel what you would feel if they were actually Here right Now.

4. Share this experience with them in whatever way feels most loving. Tell them how you feel, or simply caress their face and gaze into the windows of their soulful eyes.

These moments are as "real" as any other, and the loved one you are holding may even find themselves thinking of you or feeling more cherished. Love is always available and is never wasted when shared.

Break the old pattern of present-moment denial and present-moment resistance. Make it your practice to withdraw attention from past and future whenever they are not needed. Step out of the time dimension as much as possible in everyday life.

—The Power of Now *by Eckhart Tolle, German writer*

You, in the Passionate Now

The traditional Irish definition of eternity is not the usual sense of *endless ongoing time,* but rather an *open spacious present,* and this is what I'd like to offer you Here. A kiss, a love, a moment, or a life, experienced in this spacious present, is a priceless gift: rich, full, sweet, and deeply nourishing.

The Greeks say that there are two different kinds of time: *chronos,* or clock time, and *kyros,* or inner time, like the mutable time in dreams. It's easy to recognize that your sense of time is malleable in the dream state; you can live for years in the space of a nanosecond, an hour, or a night. What people are also beginning to discover is that clock time, or chronological time, also seems plastic. The few minutes that the dentist is drilling in your mouth may feel like forever, while a car trek on a familiar road may seem to whiz by at twice the usual pace. Time warps actually seem to exist.

One of the major variables in how we experience clock time is where on the time line we place our attention. If you're driving down the street, hurrying to arrive somewhere else, you'll more than likely experience a shortage of time, Now. The faster you hurry ahead, the faster time flies. Why? Because your attention, your sense of you, is projected ahead of where you actually are Now; you're propelling yourself into your future time. You've missed your Now, your experience of your life and passion is experienced only in the Now.

In these days of chronic multitasking, the vast majority of adults are rarely present in this time-space. When you're worrying about the future, or manipulating your reality to control a future outcome, you are not in the Now. If you're upset about something that has happened two years, two weeks, or two hours ago and are still chewing the cud of your past experience, you're clearly not in the Now. Re-masticating your experience regenerates and perpetuates the emotional trauma by re-creating your past in your Now. This leaves you gone from Here, Now, not available to love. You're too busy re-experiencing old wounds.

If we're tied up in webs of unresolved guilt or righteousness or anger, we spin this emotional tone from our past into the future and generate more of it. Our present is spent perpetuating the past. When this happens, we have no time and energy left with which to regenerate, or re-create, our experience of our life. Our life will reflect this as a personal power leakage. Dwelling in either the past or future drains us of our vital energy and leaves us more or less powerless, impotent in this moment.

Our futures are an expression of what we are feeling Now. It's a huge illusion to think that we can make ourselves feel better Now by controlling our life to guarantee certain future outcomes. You get more of what you focus your mind and feelings upon. If, in this moment, you are wanting to experience something other than *what is,* then you are perpetuating a future in which you get to experience more frustration from *what is.* Energy follows thought and is empowered by emotion.

Your point of renewal, your point of power, is in the present. Your *attention* in this moment is essential for passionate *presence*. Anything I'm rejecting blocks my presence and my ability to experience yours. To have great passion, to experience the fullness of yourself and others, you must begin by finding ways to cultivate an intimate relationship with the fullness of Now, to openly embrace *what is*. Pay attention and you will notice this directly, and then you will begin to discover the power that is yours only in present time.

Your life is currently on the menu; I invite you Here, to feel your heart's desires and feast upon all the flavors of love: spicy, sweet, dark, rich, colorful, and artfully shared.

Kiss Tips

Do not start kissing with a preprogrammed encounter in mind. Allow the kiss to happen in the fullness of just this moment.

Slow *waaay* down, at least for the opener. This is not a timid or hesitant, hovering kiss. This is a kiss that is offered fully and deeply, slowly enough that your attention is fully present in every nuance of breath, taste, pressure, and melding.

If your mind wanders and you pull your consciousness away, you will break the connection and your beloved will feel the loss of you. So bring your attention back Here, Now, and look into your partner's eyes and connect again. Allow your emotions to rush through your body, breathe greedily, and fan the fire of your passion.

How she felt when first he kissed her—like a tub of roses swimming in honey, cologne, nutmeg and blackberries.

—*Samuel Sullivan Cox,*
19th-century American writer and congressman

Opening into the Expanded Now

Try coming back into your bodily sense of self, sitting in a chair at your home or, if you have access to privacy on a beach, on the sand at the water's edge. Be in this moment, in this place, wherever you are. Feel into your body, your breath, and your environment. Relax and open your body and your mind; stop contracting. Expand your attention around you, outside of your private bubble of self. Breathe air that comes from miles away, and exhale your breath out to the heavens. Open up your relationship with space.

When you open your attention like this, you also open your experience of Now and actually have an experience of expanded time, a larger Now. You're in the spacious, timeless fullness of Now, and Now, and Now. Here, open, Now is the only "place" you can experience your power to re-create, to heal, to be inspired, to love.

Time to Swoon

According to the *Guinness Book of World Records*, the record for the most couples kissing at the same time was set by 5,122 Filipino couples on February 13, 2004. They kissed for ten seconds. Ten seconds is infinitely longer than the nanosecond peck most folks share; however, it's still just grazing the surface of the kissing moment.

1. Try the ten-second kiss first. Use a timer or clock. If no one is around to kiss, just use the palm of your hand. How well do you get connected in ten seconds?

2. Now take a few deep breaths and drop your attention into your heart, as deep and open as you can be.

3. Become fully present in your animal body, your wild heart, your open mind, and your sweet spirit. Feel your full self arrive as an offering, a precious gift for your beloved.

4. Now bring all of this focus and resonance into a kiss that lasts a *full minute*. Yes, a full minute! Challenge yourself to stay present and connected. Breathe deeply, feel yourself, your beloved, your heart, their heart. Risk swooning.

Anything worth doing is worth doing slowly.

—Gypsy Rose Lee, American burlesque performer and entertainer

Bring Me *All* of You

How long can you *be* fully Here and Now in this nuance of your experience? And in this moment Now, and this Now, and this? Your answer is the measuring stick for the depth of your intimacy potential.

Have you ever watched someone performing live and heard them drop a few musical notes, lose the thread of the script, or miss the beat? We'd say *they lost it.* What is it they lost? It is *presence*—they mentally or emotionally drifted away from Here, away from what their body was experiencing. When attention floats away for only for a split second, it's relatively easy to jump back into the moment and pick up the beat. But when we're not present for larger chunks of time, our life becomes less alive, more dull and heavy. We're not animating our life with our attention, our consciousness, our *be*-ing, or our senses, and we end up with a life of disengaged, heartless *do*-ing.

When we are not here to be found, our lovers and the world will have a hard time finding us. Being present Now in this moment is one thing; being present Here in our body on this planet is yet another axis of presence. This means having your presence consciously, sensuously in your body, feet on the ground. Everyone is familiar with the mindlessness of running on automatic pilot: the feeling of being spaced out, numb, shut down, turned off, or elsewhere.

Does this sound familiar? You mentally trot down the aisles of the grocery store wondering what to make for dinner as you're driving along the freeway at 70 miles an hour; then you suddenly bolt back into the driver's seat, wondering if you missed your exit and grateful that you didn't wander into the car beside you. You make mental lists of things to do while your partner is talking to you, or cogitate on an email that needs sending while you dress your children for day care. You may eat your meals while directing your attention to the TV, barely engaged with your family or even with what you see, feel, or taste. You may fantasize about someone else while you're kissing and being sexual "with" your partner. My heart breaks as I write that. With you being elsewhere, the quality of your life and love suffers greatly. By trying to be everywhere out there, you end up nowhere, empty of Now Here. You remain unseen, untouched; you feel unloved, isolated in a disconnected existence.

The price you pay for this lack of presence is actually astounding. You don't feel the energy of the planet as you drive down the road, and you miss taking delight in nature's seasons, in the changing light, in the dance of clouds and shadows. You miss looking into the eyes of your children as they are talking with you, and your kids begin to feel that they are just another task on your list of things to get done. Without heartful presence, you miss exploring the rich possibilities of artful loving and deep communion with your beloved. You miss experiencing the full-color, 3-D version of life.

Arriving in the Body

When we're feeling disconnected from the experience of our body, our mental energy is usually disengaged from the subtle energy circuitry of the body-mind. When this happens, the cellular intelligence of the body goes stupid, and our relationship to our body dulls. Moving the body in an intentional, rhythmic pattern while breathing deeply will go a long way toward reconnecting body and mind, bringing an increased energy flow and function to both. Viagra would go out of business if people knew how to activate the energy in their bodies!

Here's an exercise that can get you started on realizing your body's energy. Pay close attention to your walking pattern as you head out for a stroll. Notice where the motion of your walking begins. Do your knees lift as though you are on a marionette's string, plopping one foot down and pitching you forward? What are your arms doing? Is your head leading the walk, propelling yourself ahead into the future?

Learn to walk using your whole body, in a flowing synchrony of cross-patterned arm and leg action. Begin your step's motion *from the hip,* swinging it out with your leg following along, and plant that foot. Allow the motion of the hip-first momentum to flow through the upper and lower body, with arms swinging in counter position to the legs. Now combine the walking with deep, diaphragmatic breathing. You may feel a little like you're marching, but once this rhythm gets flowing you'll find that it activates a burst of energy and cultivates ease and grace in your gait.

With this simple cross-patterning of your limbs, combined with deep breathing, you will encourage a vibrant brain-body-heart conversation and begin to weave yourself into the Here and Now.

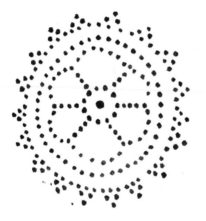

There is a vitality, a life force, an energy, a quickening, that is translated through you into action, and because there is only one of you in all time, this expression is unique. And if you block it, it will never exist through any other medium and will be lost.

—Martha Graham, American dancer and choreographer

Gifts of Presence, Masculine and feminine

*f*eeling awake, vibrant, aware, charged, intense, charismatic, potent, quick, brilliant, tuned in, and turned on are all aspects of the quality of *presence*. Being fully connected to this space and this time, this Here and Now—that's where presence lives.

Masculine and *feminine energies* show up as different styles of presence. This Here and Now can be experienced like a focused laser, a penetrating masculine energy, or like a 250-watt lightbulb, the full, open radiance of feminine energy. While our personalities all include both masculine and feminine energies, we usually have more of one than the other—and our dominant energy may or may not match our gender. We always have a choice as to which aspect of our sexual energy we want to animate, and we are usually more comfortable with the dominant flavor. When we fully animate our dominant sexual energy style, we feel more bodaciously ourselves, alive and connected from the inside out.

Masculine Presence

The recognition of the masculine-style, laser-focused presence is why we hush when a golfer takes his stance on the green; it's why we hold our breath as the rock climber scales high above us or the race car zooms around a tight corner. Masculine energy animates this intensely goal-oriented style of presence, which delights in pushing its focus to the extreme in sports and daring challenges. Masculine energy revels in penetrating deeply into the moment, free from all other distraction. In the arts of loving, this passionate focus is best expressed as ravishment: a hungry, deep savoring of the time together. Masculine energy penetrates your heart and your lips, right through your skin and into your soul. The strong, grounded resonance of masculine presence is what is most sexy to those with a feminine essence.

When a masculine person is racing ahead of himself, he loses his presence, leaving his partner behind. Rarely does he know how much this hurts: he has not merged with his beloved, and intimacy has been broken. When he's not connected to his heart and that of his beloved, his attentions can easily become ravagement instead of ravishment. Drop the hesitations that keep you second-guessing your past, masculine lovers, and drop the goal orientations that keep you in the future. Bring yourself back to the love that is available in this moment: feel into your partner's heart, take a few deep breaths, and appreciate something about your beloved. Re-engage in the deep, rich journey of the eternal present, and love will fill your life.

Scarlett, you need kissing badly. That's what's wrong with you. You should be kissed and often, and by someone who knows how.

—**Gone with the Wind,** *by Margaret Mitchell, American writer*

feminine Presence

The feminine style of presence is like a charged, open field of brilliance, often in movement. Feminine sexual energy is easy to recognize in the open passion of skilled ice skaters, electrified dancers, and jamming jazz musicians. They're opening their focus to access the emotional energy that enlivens their hearts, moves their bodies, and animates their creative spirit.

The artists are opening, surrendering to a rich, wide fullness of Now, in living color, resonant sound waves, precision of gesture, and full-throttle emotion. This opening into a large embrace of life force, in the Now, earthy and in the body, is the feminine aspect of presence. She surrenders, open, to be penetrated by the focused presence of the masculine, like a cell opening to the penetration of sperm, like a basket receiving a ball. His appreciation opens her walls; she relaxes in the affection of his embrace. She melts with the fullness of his kiss and moans with release as her heart is swept ever wider open. The more his loving presence penetrates her depths, the more open and radiant she feels, the more the masculine energy is attracted.

Developing the Presence

asculine energy is cultivated by learning to call yourself fully into the bodily presence—for instance, via sports that challenge your focus and reliability.

Feminine sexual energy is cultivated by some form of ecstasy in the body, which could be any activity that brings a bodily sense of heightened life force: dancing, tending the garden, walking in the woods, swimming in the ocean, practicing yoga, enjoying a good massage, or cooking a sumptuous meal.

In both cases there is a deep necessity to be fully present, with both the mind and the emotions woven into the bodily experience.

Kiss Tips

A deep kiss is not one that has your tongue in your partner's mouth, probing for tonsils; it's a deep merging of your energy with your partner's and can be conveyed with the simplest of gestures if felt deeply. Most often we can pay attention to that level only when we really slow down, as if we are in slow motion, allowing for palpable tenderness and lots of breathing to keep the charge alive. Moving fully into this moment, your energy expands and penetrates into your partner's being as they open, surrendering to the sweetness of the moment. Your lips are conversing in a language of their own, both surrendered and potent, demanding and willing.

She lifted her face suddenly to him, and he touched it with his lips.
So cold, so fresh, so sea-clear her face was, it was like kissing a flower
that grows near the surf.

————Women in Love, *by D. H. Lawrence, British writer*

Opening to the Senses

Opening to the earthy, physical senses is one of the simplest ways to reconnect with your bodily experience, Here and Now. Awareness and permission are the keys. Instead of thinking about your experience, drop your consciousness into your body and sense it directly. Really *feel* every nuance of what goes on in your shower, the pulse and heat of the water as it melts away tensions and raises gooseflesh on your thighs. Indulge in a pair of exfoliating shower gloves and some triple-milled French soap, and luxuriate in the fragrance and friction as you scrub away the day's accumulation of stress and debris. Encourage such luscious moments.

Can you take that state of luxurious nurturing into the dinner that is cooking in your kitchen? Let yourself fully arrive in the present as you walk into the room and savor the aroma. Let yourself savor your own delight as well; this amplifies your experience. Really appreciate the visual splendor of your favorite meal coming out of the oven. Serve it up generously. Do you taste the first bite, deciding whether to season it, and then forget to taste it after that? Try building your sensual attention: expand your bliss tolerance a bit, and stay as sensually present as possible for as long as possible. Can you actually taste the whole meal? Now extend this sensual savoring into several minutes of breathy kissing, hands stroking face and hair, inhaling every scent.

Once you learn to experience your senses one at a time, you can learn to become multisensual: feel the texture of the earth underfoot as you walk in nature, smell the air, groove on the sounds of the critters or water lapping on the shore, enjoy the various shades of all the colors around you, feel the variance of temperature on your face as you pass through the sun and shade while breathing diaphragmatically. You'll become so alive, grounded in a fullness of *what is.* It's this quality of aliveness focused in the Here and Now that is required of an artful lover, the vital prerequisite for a moment of boundaryless intimacy, a rich repast of lip and tongue.

LESSON 2

Relax and Open Up

I dreamt my lady came and found me dead. . .
And breathed such life with kisses in my lips,
That I revived, and was an emperor.

—**Romeo and Juliet**, *by William Shakespeare,*
16th-century English dramatist and poet

Stressed Love

Stress management is no longer an optional undertaking, as it was when I began creating a stress management program for a large Seattle hospital in 1977. The ever-increasing pace of life chronically demands that we race through our days and nights, often leaving behind all that is not deemed essential for survival. This race for the finish often robs us of the moments that are most comforting, peaceful, and restorative. With no respite from this pace, these escalating tensions will wreak havoc with our intimate lives.

Life's tensions block sensation and cultivate splits in the body-mind, walling you off from the warmth of your heart. The body trains itself to remember what you experience as the norm. We generate habits that are inertial, that tend to keep on keeping on. Our patterns of breathing, muscular or joint tensions, and vocal, emotional, and mental habits all persist until we intentionally *do* or *be* something different. Habits of multitasking and pushing on from one strategic task to another bind your attention to the surface of life, denying you access to the spacious depths of your passionate, wise, and radiant spirit. Your Inner Lover thrives in these deep, open spaces. Your particular habits of openness or closure will determine how large a surrender into love you will claim.

When we've been living life stressfully, it's common to try to deal with the intensity by going even faster, thinking that maybe we can get it over with sooner, or get more completed quicker. This rarely works; instead, we spin ourselves into a tight, fast-moving orbit that feels very *self*-enclosed. Eventually we forget how to relax, forget how to live a luscious life, how to embrace the moment and the loved ones in it.

Once you're this stuck in your inertia, it's hard to do anything else. If you try to relax, you find yourself pacing around, fidgeting, wondering what to do; or else you fall asleep. There seems to be no middle ground in which we are fully present and awake and yet comfortably softened, breathing deeply, relaxed, open and connected to our experience. We've forgotten how to let go and simply *be* in our bodies, and how to *be* in a life that offers some freedom and grace and balance. We need this comfortable, spacious platform on which to create a lovingly intimate life, so we may be open with each other.

Simply Let Go

Come back to the freedom of resting in the moment. Simply stop for a few minutes. Be silent and allow all your mental, emotional, and physical tensions to fall from within you into the ground. As you concentrate on releasing the tension, take a deep breath in, and then exhale. Repeat for several deep breaths, letting go just a bit more with each exhalation. *Sssiiiigh* . . .

This simple exercise of letting go may seem basic, but it's worth incorporating into your daily life. We need to cultivate new habits of renewal to break up the inertia of stress. Practice using the "between" moments to let go, moments when you're stalled in the midst of your to-do list (e.g., waiting at the stoplight, in line at the market, getting a haircut, or riding in an elevator). You'll feel less burdened, and lighter.

We find rest in those we love, and we provide a resting place in ourselves for those who love us.

—*Saint Bernard of Clairvaux, 12th-century French monk*

Head Strong

The face, head, neck, and shoulders hold much of the body's tension. Our ears gradually begin to squinch down into hunching shoulders as our necks contract with tightening muscles. Chests tighten and collapse, breathing shrinks, necks lock, shoulders ache, and the head booms away like a radio receiving six stations. You know the feeling?

This experience of being "uptight" helps to keep your attention in your head and away from your emotional heart and sexual energy, anything felt below the neck. As a culture, we've declared that mental activity is of primary importance. The body's wisdom and emotional intelligence are not important, society says, so close them down and shift that energy supply to the head. This energy dynamic is one of our biggest blocks to experiencing passion.

For both men and women, a deep relaxation needs to happen in order to open to the flow of emotion and that deep, sweet Inner Lover who resides in our hearts and spirit. Intimacy cannot develop in a state of walled-off, locked-up energy flow. Our intimate experience gets pinched off, and we are left sharing *ideas* about reality but not our direct intimate experience. Without breaking the stress cycles, the body eventually forgets how to relax. Those inner experiences require an open, flowing energy system resonating with the hormonal responses activated by the rush of emotional stimulation. Unclenching and letting go is essential for re-establishing a conscious experience of our deep feelings, impulses, and desires. Passion rushes through open systems.

Ten Commandments for Reducing Stress

The load of tension we carry in our body is often not only the stress of too much physical work but also the attitudes with which we approach our work, life, and relationships. These commandments for reducing stress are a powerful little list of attitude adjustments given to me by a friend several years ago, written by an anonymous author. You may find that they break a few of your inner rules. Consider the potential payoff from breaking those rules and buying yourself a little freedom.

1. Thou shalt not be perfect, nor try to be.
2. Thou shalt not try to be all things to all people.
3. Thou shalt occasionally leave things undone, including things that ought to be done.
4. Thou shalt not spread thyself too thin.
5. Thou shalt learn to say no when it's best for you.
6. Thou shalt schedule alone time for thyself.
7. Thou shalt switch off and do nothing at regular intervals.
8. Thou shalt at times be boring, inelegant, untidy, and unattractive.
9. Thou shalt not feel guilty.
10. Thou shalt not be thine own worst enemy but instead thine own best friend.

Intentional Rest

One thing I have found to be helpful for myself and my students is incorporating elements of hatha yoga into my daily routine. Hatha yoga practices are exercises designed to open and integrate the body, breath, and presence—a wonderfully healing thing to do. While many people find themselves too tight and filled with tension to practice many of the standard yoga postures, there is a whole series of restorative poses that are simple and regenerative (see Exercise 2.2).

Other ways to achieve intentional rest: Buy books or audiotapes that teach you how to let go, breathe deeply, or meditate. Take classes in stretching and stress management. See how much more loving you become. Practice these arts of letting go with your partner, then spend some time kissing after your relaxation tape is over. Make purring sounds and savor your softer, more open selves.

Waiting in the Exhale

Take ten minutes and see what a little intentional rest can do.

1. Begin by lying down at the edge of a wall, on a blanket or carpet, with your buttocks touching the wall and your legs resting up against it. Arms and hands rest out to the side. (Alternatively, you can use the couch, with your calves on the seat cushions, lying in front of it, thighs against it.)

2. Breathe deeply and allow yourself to count while you inhale.

3. Now exhale slowly and fully, doubling that count.

4. Rest between breaths in that still pause at the end of the exhalation.

5. Continue this for ten to fifteen minutes.

6. Slide your legs down from the wall (or couch), roll to your side, and turn to place your back against the wall for several breaths, savoring the changes. See how much of this restfulness you can carry with you into your next moments.

Love is the great miracle cure. Loving ourselves works miracles
in our lives.

—Louise Hay, American writer

Low Bliss Tolerance

Anhedonia, or "the inability to gain pleasure from normally pleasurable experiences," was first identified in the 1890s and is now often considered by many psychotherapists to be a component of depression. I have found anhedonia to be rampant in Western culture. Of course it's depressing to live a life without experiencing pleasure, and we do it to ourselves. We have been trained to focus on defending ourselves from what we fear. We cultivate habits of attention that are actually focused on missing what is enjoyable and life affirming, because we're busy making sure that what we don't want isn't showing up.

We're so strongly focused on what is *wrong* in our lives that we've overpowered the sensory messages of what is pleasant and enjoyable. This lack of celebration, of appreciation, happens regularly and often. You can be going through your day and having several tasks that are going well, and not even notice that your day is going well. However, when something takes a turn for the worse, you get all stirred up and upset and tell the story of your disappointment over and over, adding on other things like it from the past that have happened in your life, and then projecting even more miserable events into your future. Bit by bit, our negative experiences loom large, while the pleasure in life gets ignored and eventually not even experienced—hence the inability to experience pleasure from normally pleasurable experiences. We're too busy focusing on what is wrong with our experience.

One of the several problems with cultivating the inability to experience pleasure is that we become suspicious when something lovely comes our way. We believe it's too good to be true, so we wait for the other shoe to drop, for it to hurt us, or for it to go away and leave us wounded because it didn't stay forever. I wonder, how *can* this loveliness be true, or renewing, or lasting, when we're not even letting ourselves experience it fully?

Two people with similar stress loads but different ways of handling stress can take a walk along a deserted beach and return from the walk in completely different states of Being. One can fuss and fume all the way down the beach and arrive back with all the reasons this or that is wrong in their life, and a list of what needs to happen to make it right. That person returns filled with anxiety and frustration, having barely noticed that they were on a beach.

Meanwhile, the other beach walker takes deep breaths, releases their mental grip, feels into their body, digs their feet into the sand. They begin to "arrive" in the Here and Now, smell the beach scent, and feel their hips begin to loosen. Their breath drops down and opens them up. Weight falls from their shoulders, and arms join the rhythm of hips in a sense of freedom and release. They arrive back at the landing feeling open, lighter, connected through their body to a direct experience of *what is,* Here and Now. They have been bathed by beauty, fresh air, and the rhythms of waves and walking.

Conversing with Life

Luxuriate in the freedom of simple moments. Allow lots of time to do a simple task, stay focused with an open and playful presence, and allow yourself to luxuriate in the details of the task. When watering the garden, I like to hold an inner conversation with the leaves, budding flowers, ground, and sky. "Oh, you say you'd like some fertilizer? Kelp meal you say? Why yes, I'll pick some up. And you're loving that sunshine, aren't you?"

Adoring a pot of fragrant lilies or giving your old car a word of encouragement helps you build a more conscious and intentional relationship with life.

When we converse with life, life converses with us, and we find more depth and enrichment flowing into our experience and begin to drop our walls of lonely isolation.

A soft lip would tempt you to an eternity of kissing.

—Ben Jonson, 16th-century English dramatist and poet

Stiff Upper Lip

Tense kissing is agony; we really suffer from tight-lipped, unyielding kisses. They feel impersonal and cold. Tension builds walls. Tense lips and a tense body cut us off from what we're feeling and experiencing. The kiss becomes a flat and off-putting experience—frustrating, hard surfaces meeting and generating even more tension. A head, shoulder, back, or foot massage may make the difference between kissing each other's walls and contacting your soul. Release your tension, cultivate the art of letting go (see Exercise 2.1), and begin to expand your bliss tolerance.

One sure barrier to luscious kissing is the stiff upper lip. Oftentimes emotional tension thins the lip to such an extent that it seems to disappear altogether, causing a mashing of his mustache into her tender face, or a bashing of their teeth as she searches for the fullness of his lip and love.

Sadly, many cultures encourage those with predominantly masculine energy to cultivate the emotional toughness that one develops by "keeping a stiff upper lip." And even sadder for those with mainly feminine energy, the dominating masculine paradigm often demands that they too engage in this act of bravado, which masks the emotional flow of their energy. Stiff lippers often find themselves embittered, hardened, and cut off from their wide emotional range.

Your Stiff Upper Lip

See what you notice about the energy habits you carry in your lips, face, breath, gut, and heart. Intentionally stiffen your upper lip, slowly enough so that you can notice what happens in your body-mind and in your emotional flow. Now exaggerate the stiffness and make all the bizarre faces that come with the stiffening. Notice what happens in your breath, in your gut, and in your heart.

Gimme Some Lip!

This kind of focused practice brings fresh learning right into the cellular memory of the lips because so much of your consciousness is reprogramming the experience, in the Now. Gradually the cellular memory habits generated in the past will be overwritten by the intentionality of freedom and the flowing, loving energy that is being shared in current time. This exercise can be done alone, at any time, by simply using your own lips and tongue to suckle and encourage fullness and relaxation in them. Your lips will learn to love loving.

If you have a kissing partner, try kissing each other with the stiff upper lip (see previous exercise). How satisfying is it? What's being held back in that tension?

Now focus on relaxing, and begin to gently caress your partner's upper lip between your own two. Alternate between the top and the lower lip, embracing and massaging tenderly, strongly, tugging hungrily, playfully, and with heartful awareness. Bring your tongue into this play and get creative.

Remember to breathe deeply, dropping your breath and awareness into your belly to open the tension that's held in the front of your body.

The most powerful symptom of love is a tenderness which becomes at times almost insupportable.

—Victor Hugo, 19th-century French writer and poet

Be-foreplay

R emember that the whole day is foreplay for loving, and you will only be able to deliver the loving when you've been cultivating its presence in your body. Your chronic tension patterns are the prison bars of your Inner Lover. Tension in the body will decrease the flow of energy and block the subtle currents of flow and movement that you need to feel in order to artfully circulate passionate energy. Get good massages, practice yoga, or do frequent stretching of any kind. You actually have to wake yourself up in the midst of holding on in order to free yourself.

We must move our attention and breath into our body's old habits in order to re-create them. In the midst of a massage, try not to chatter, either out loud or in your head. Bring your complete attention inside your body and feel into the tensions, sensations, and releases happening within your tissues. Breathe deeply, especially when confronted with the tender ache of blocked energy in your body, as this will bring the tissues what they need to regenerate a healthy charge. Remember that the message of pain, any pain, is "send energy here." Practice developing sensitivity to your internal energy as it courses through you or feels lumped in your shoulders, as it releases and rushes through your spine. Ride the flow, feeling into it as if you were on a surfboard. The energetic charge of your attention, breath, and heartfelt compassion for your body is a natural healing balm.

In our daily life, we radiate what we experience. If we're tense, we radiate tension, infecting the people and situations of our life with this dis-ease. Even if you're trying to do good, that goodness will be resonating with your underlying tensions. Once you have relaxed, opened, and fully returned to your own body, you'll naturally vibrate with deeper, more potent and passionate energies. By allowing yourself to be loved open, both by your own compassionate presence and by your permission for the bodywork to lovingly relax you, you've become available to love; you will be lovable. The frequency of this vibrant, warm, and open presence will then become the gift you share with your beloved, your family, and your community. By loving yourself, you become lovable, and this lovability allows others to love and feel lovable as well. Good deal!

Hand-to-Body Rejuvenation

Many studies have documented the necessity of a mother's touch to infants, but we don't outgrow the need for touch when we are weaned. Touch deprivation is rampant these days. We habitually hold ourselves away from each other in a gesture of political correctness. We're more likely to pet the animals around us than the people we love. I find this totally bizarre, for there's nothing more soothing to a stressed-out human than to be touched.

Couples massages are a wonderful way to cultivate intimacy. Whether it's a ten-minute shoulder rub, a foot massage, or a full body meltdown that lasts for hours, a massage opens us to the possibility of being more present and receptive to a deeper sharing. We relax, our breath and tense body expand, the awareness in our skin is revivified, and we feel much more "in touch." (See Basic Massage Tips on page 74.)

We kiss. And it feels like we have just shrugged off the world.

—*Jim Shahin, American writer*

Learn to Luxuriate

You will find that, if asked, the body will often invite you to move and stretch in certain unexpected directions. This is what I call spontaneous yoga, and it is a wonderful way of developing a responsive relationship with your impulses. Directly ask your body how it wants to stretch, then listen by moving into that posture. Feel it deeply. Keep the mind focused encouragingly within the body, and incorporate deep breathing during the stretch, as this will open the door to new possibilities of energy flow and vitality.

Pay attention to the way the animals around you move. We've almost forgotten that we, too, are animal creatures. Critters have no sense of disconnection from their bodies. They're not reading magazines as their body runs on a machine. Dogs engage their whole body happily as they lope into the lake after a ball, or jump for the Frisbee, or collapse onto the most comfortable sunny spot. No self-respecting cat gets up without a full-body stretch, and when cats need to be fondled, they will insist that you cooperate. As they luxuriate in their bodies, animals can teach you how to keep a thread of your own consciousness in your body. Let them help you remember to get up from your desk every hour, so you can shake yourself off, as if you'd just jumped out of the lake with the ball in your mouth. Let them also remind you to purr when petted and to shake your booty when you're really happy! Then try stretching with your partner and luxuriating in some loose and languid kissing. Breathe deeply and purr.

Basic Massage Tips

When you're massaging your beloved during a pause in a busy day, it's a good idea to begin with the head, neck, and shoulders. We store much of the day's accumulated stress in our heads, especially around our eyes. We clamp our necks and shoulders in order to maintain a lot of charge in the head, which separates us from the experience of our body. Regaining this connection of energy flow is essential if we're to experience anything much in our body, either physically or emotionally. So begin massaging your partner's shoulders, neck, and head as if they were one cold lump of clay you wanted to warm and soften.

If, after the upper body has been massaged, you've got time and energy for more, then ask what your partner would most like to receive. Back and foot massages are great, but they may have a pain in their knee or hands that are tight. Let them decide, then do your best to open your heart, relax, and knead them into comfort and flow.

Begin your massage with lighter, softer strokes and eventually move into deeper layers of tension. Use a skin lubricant on their bare skin so you don't create friction burns. If you don't have massage oil at hand, use a little cooking oil, such as olive oil. Remind them to breathe deeply and let go. You also need to breathe deeply as you massage to keep your energy circulating and grounded. Ask for feedback from your partner: Is this too much pressure or not enough? More time here on this spot, or move on? When you're ready to finish, again return to soft, light strokes, as if you're lifting out the tension and smoothing out their ruffled fur. Wash your hands afterward, intentionally washing away the tension your body may have picked up from your partner. If it feels right, negotiate a massage trade after they've rested a bit.

Then I did the simplest thing in the world.

I leaned down . . . and kissed him.

And the world cracked open.

—Agnes de Mille, American choreographer and dancer

Be Relentless in Letting Go

Our immune system is seriously compromised after twenty-four hours of unrelenting stress. We need breaks every day to recalibrate our body's response to stressful living. But life is not going to stop so you can take a break. That's why it's important to relax your mind with a bit of quiet, or exercise your body with activity, on a regular basis.

Honoring small completions is a way to break up the day so we can have a sense of satisfaction between the endless lists of tasks. Finished the dishes? Don't immediately start running down your list of what's not yet accomplished. Savor what is finished. Enjoy the shine on those dishes as you put them in the cupboard. Feel the peace of mind that comes with a completed task. Tension is contagious, as are relaxation and well-being. Offer yourself small moments of contentment and peace of mind throughout the day, and you'll have a full bucket to bring to the love of your life.

LESSON 3

Become One

Soul meets soul on lovers' lips.

—*Percy Bysshe Shelley, 19th-century English Romantic poet*

With You Lying Next to Me I feel Lonely

I've been a psychotherapist for almost twenty-five years, and I've heard a lot of talk these last few decades about cultivating people with strong boundaries, their own separate sense of Self, and the necessary walls to protect them. But I've also been psychic since I was a child, and I've never seen one of these boundary lines in anyone's energy—so to me this theory, like so many others, seems a little askew.

In relationships, codependency is out and independence is in, so that we can be whole, on our own. We're told to balance our masculine and feminine energies so we can do anything the other gender can do. Women are encouraged to have compelling careers and learn to fix the car. Men are told to nurture, have feelings, and clean the house. Eventually people find themselves in a relationship in which each person has their own friends, their own interests, their own bank accounts, their own therapist, their own orgasms, and their own lives, separate from their partner's. Couples are taught to trade favors so they can both get their *needs* met: I'll do this to you if you'll do that to me. A relationship becomes a business transaction, a deal between two separate sets of boundaries. Is it any wonder that couples feel more and more estranged these days, wondering where the intimacy, passion, and love have gone? Are there ways to stay connected while learning to be whole?

Deeper than the career, deeper than the ability to clean house or fix the car, deeper than a willingness to sit through a performance because your partner wants you to be there, is the realm of the heart: the deep heart, the land of the Inner Lover. This aspect of human nature is all too readily ignored in the busy lives of modern adults, and it is felt only in extraordinary moments, like the first time you knew you loved your partner, or the moment they asked you to join their life, or the first moments of gazing upon your newborn babe. In these powerful experiences we shift our attention out of our heads, away from all the to-do lists and the business of life, and into something deep within. We touch the spirit of love that dwells within us all the time, waiting to be felt.

It takes experiences to draw us into the realm of the heart, so now that we have read about how to be present, in the Here and Now, we'll focus more on experientially merging within ourselves, with life itself, and with each other. To that end, this chapter contains more exercises than talk, more moments of engaging the deeper aspects of ourselves so we can learn to cultivate this wellspring of warmth and togetherness. In these depths we find the common ground of love, the energy of passion, and the uplifting fullness of Being. In this realm there are no boundaries, no walls, and nothing to protect; you are one with all the energies of life. This Oneness is the essence of who we deeply are; it's the spirit of life itself that threads together every living thing.

Practice these exercises alone and with your partner. Learn to go deep within yourself and each other, and you'll build a foundation of togetherness that will ignite your ability to love at any time, wherever you are, right in the midst of life—whether you're cleaning house, working in the world, or mowing the lawn.

What greater thing is there for two human souls than to feel that they are joined . . . to strengthen each other . . . to be one with each other in silent unspeakable memories?

—*George Eliot, 19th-century English writer*

One Plus One Equals One

We cultivate intimacy by letting down the walls between what seems to be inside of us and what seems to be outside, between what seems to be a separate You and a separate Me. The quantum sciences have established quite clearly that no real boundaries exist between anyone or anything on this planet, and yet we humans seem to feel the need to draw lines in our minds and in our hearts and in the sand. This practice of dividing keeps us wrestling with conflicting feelings about being separate—feeling safer within our crystallized self, even while other parts of us are feeling compelled by a deep urge to merge.

When you are busy *doing life,* you separate yourself from your experience and create the tension of a fundamental disconnect. If you shift to a *living of life* rather than a *doing of life,* you will find a greater sense of ease within yourself. This attitudinal difference creates a shift in the quality of your attention; you are weaving yourself and your life together. In this embrace of your life, you will be receiving energy back from life rather than pouring your energy into a black hole. You will be nourished, and several layers of stress will simply melt away, allowing you to feel more deeply the joy that is at the heart of your Being.

Fire Gazing (Concentration Practice)

Simple meditations give us time to gather ourselves and reclaim our sense of Here and Now. Focusing our visual attention stills the mind and has the effect of gathering us from our scattered attentions into a single focus, *becoming one* within. We can rejoin, relax, and renew ourselves very simply.

Candle gazing is a basic meditation, quickly learned, and is a satisfying way to call yourself into this moment, refocus your attention, and weave together your scattered energies. You may choose a flower, a crystal, a tree, or any favorite object to focus upon, but the slight changes in the color and dance of a candle flame can engage the wandering mind more readily than something that is still.

1. Sit quietly before an open flame, candle, or fireplace.

2. Take a moment to ground your energy by contracting the muscles in your pelvic floor (the muscles you use to hold back your excretory functions) as you inhale, and relaxing them as you exhale. This pulls charge away from your head and down into your body, weaving you together energetically.

3. Feel your environment around you, and your connection to the planet.

4. Take several deep breaths, settling yourself.

5. Drop all thoughts from your mind.

6. Allow your eyes to fall upon the flame.

7. As thoughts appear in your mind, drop them and refocus on the flame.

8. Return again and again and lose yourself in the flame, not analyzing, not expecting, simply opening more and more, allowing your system to recalibrate.

9. After ten to thirty minutes, close your eyes and notice everything you feel.

10. Allow a strand of your awareness to continue experiencing the sensations in your body as you return to your day.

You too must mingle my friends
since the earth and the sky
are mingled just for you and me.

—Rumi, 13th-century Persian mystic

Hugging Arts

A hug from a dear friend, a child, an elder, or a beloved can be a stiff, duty-bound, halfhearted, tense moment, or it can be a magical event filled with streams of warmth within a tender embrace. With all the hugging going on these days, which hugs feel most nourishing? Some hugs are A-framed—shoulders embracing, with pelvises held apart. These usually come with the dreaded pat-pat-pat on the back. The A-frame, or tent hug, generally leaves you feeling as though your body is off limits to touch, to be kept away from loving energy. You are left with an unsettling sense that bodies are dangerous or naughty.

Hugging tight, buff bodies often feels like hugging an ironing board; add stiff arms pulling you in, and it's the hug of the robot. All that armoring can really block the flow of warmth and tenderness. On the opposite side of the stiff tension patterns are the people who collapse upon you like a wounded rag doll, dumping all of their heavy mood into your body. Uggghh! These hugs feel like such a release to the rag doll that they tend to go on way too long, but to pull away can cause the collapsed one to fall completely: hug bondage!

The Embrace of Love

Hugging—great hugging—can be easily and quickly learned because the experience is so immediate and satisfying that we don't often resist it. Small shifts in your hugging habits can create an entirely different experience. Restructure that pat-pat-pat into a fondling of their back that soothes and enfolds, and watch your partner relax and open to you. Let your touch carry the energy of your heart, and feel their tension melt away as they snuggle into your embrace.

Reorganize that energetic collapse into a melting sensation and—*voilà!*—the hug shifts from an energy dump into a welcoming embrace of soft edges. Instead of downloading your mood upon your partner, shift your attention away from your woes and climb into your beloved's skin to find their feelings. Notice the tension patterns in them, and see if small shifts in the style of your embrace or your breathing will release them. Your energy flow will increase because it is following your attention, making it easier to feel their heart. Meet them there, in their heart, with your feelings for them.

Breathing deeply while hugging makes all the difference. It's amazing how many people hold their breath when hugging. Deep breathing allows a relaxation within the embrace and generates a flow of energy between you. Allow yourself to really *feel* your feelings in the midst of the embrace. You weave yourselves together with this energy. This merging is what makes hugging, loving, or kissing a healing experience. We become whole in each other's embrace when we are wholly present.

Here, loving love,

You and I look at each other.

—Yosano Akiko, 19th-century Japanese Romantic poet

Eye to Eye

Our eyes play a major role in loving. The quality of our gaze speaks volumes. We can look at our partner in such a way that we distance them from us, actually push them away with our eyes. Similarly, we can gather them into us with a come-hither look. Soften your eyes, relax your analyzing mind, and simply allow yourself to see and be seen. The eyes may be the windows to the soul, but most of the time we're walking around with the shades drawn. Let the shades fall away, and allow the light of your soul to shine as you look upon your lover and your world. Lovers ache to really be seen, and to be embraced in that seeing. It's so much easier to see each other when you have your lights on, yes?

Energetically, the body is said to be divided into masculine and feminine halves, masculine on the right and feminine on the left. When you are gazing at your partner, you can use this difference intentionally. Looking from your right eye into your partner's right eye stimulates the masculine side of the body and brain, for instance, and tends to cultivate the energy of *challenge*. In the midst of a Scrabble game, this could be a potent and playful gaze. In loving moments, you'd probably want to engage the left eye, which nurtures the feminine energy of connection (see Exercise 3.2).

I C U, I B U

Intentional gazing is a wonderful practice for building a depth
of connection and trust between lovers. Practice often, whenever
you feel a desire to reconnect. By deeply seeing your beloved, and
being seen by them, you're energetically weaving yourself into each
other, cultivating Oneness.

Position yourselves so that you may look easily into each other's
eyes. Allow your attention to focus mostly in your left eye. Gaze
into each other's left eye. Breathe deeply in synch with each other.
After five minutes, alternate breathing patterns so that one of you is
exhaling while the other is receiving that breath on their inhalation.
Trade breaths, energy, love, and awe.

Try a Little Tenderness

Tenderness is a natural tool for practicing the art of communion. Tenderness engenders a sense of safety and comfort in which we can rest openly. When touching our beloved tenderly, we may actually feel their presence melting into us through our skin.

Lavishly and tenderly enjoy the surfaces of each other, and then feel even deeper into and through your partner's skin, past their resistances, into their heart. Breathe deeply and savor this for some time, for this touch of hand, of cheek, of neck can be a touch as passionate as ever two lips shared. Feel both yourself and the attentions of your partner. Become exquisitely present, Here and Now; you don't want to miss this. Moments shared within this open-hearted timelessness are precious beyond measure.

Continue this exercise by spending some time caressing and nuzzling with your beloved while in the spacious energy of tenderness. Breathe deeply, lingering. Let yourself actually feel your desire to be intimate, to merge with your partner, opening yourself to them. Feel into your body as the fullness of your breath stretches the tension in your chest and belly. Notice the stirrings of warm energy rushing through you as you surrender your illusions of a solid self. Melt, and breathe. Melt, and breathe. Bring your focus into your body and allow your senses to open. Slow way down; be as slow as you need to be in order to fully sense the textures and temperatures your skin is enjoying. Smell the fragrances of their skin, their hair, their pheromones. *Inhaaaale.*

Oh, they loved dearly; their souls kissed, they kissed with their eyes,
they were both but one single kiss!

——*Heinrich Heine, 19th-century German poet*

Appreciation Weaves Us Together

As we share what we experience and enjoy in the presence of our beloved, we open our hearts and offer our enjoyments as gifts. Acknowledgment, gratitude, cherishing with words and gestures, and basic thankfulness are very loving gestures. These practices amplify and expand the gift we're offering, because we inoculate our partner with our loving energy and they vibrate as love. Cherishing your beloved with your words sends your heart's message directly, and the frequency of your loving energy reverberates right through your partner. In this moment you are vibrating in similar patterns and you experience communion. Bit by bit, tendrils of acceptance weave you together.

Love Notes

It's often easier to share what we hold dear if we write it down first. Write small love notes to your beloved often, and tell them what you love about them. Each statement is an embrace of their being.

Some examples:

I love how your eyes open and soften as you look over at me.
I'm tickled by the way you always put your tools in their favorite spot.
I swoon at the shape of your foot.
I grin seeing you collecting agates on the beach with such passion and glee.

Cultivating the Energy of Oneness

As you and your partner begin building a deeper rapport with each other, you'll become more sensitive to each other's energy flows. Cultivate these connections; learn to read them so you can navigate the rolls of emotion and the swells of heart. Learning the art of energy reading cultivates an intimate awareness of your beloved and is a path to love sublime.

Stand a few feet away from your beloved and slowly begin moving toward them. You may feel electricity, vibrations, or density in the air around them. Feel their energy as you move toward them. If you feel their energy close down, stop moving. This is a defensive move, and you will either see or feel some recoiling in them. Some subtle cues are that their facial expression may harden or you may sense them "shrinking," taking up less room, or "standing at a distance," even though they have not physically moved. This is a signal that you need to rebuild a rapport that they can trust and relax into.

Begin to reconnect with them by matching their breathing pattern and feeling into them. Actually attune your energy to match theirs through your breath and emotions. You're becoming one.

When they relax and open to you, continue to move slowly into their space, enfold them in your embrace, and kiss them with your whole self. Continue reading your partner, and adjust your embrace or kiss to their cycles of closing and opening.

Share a full-bodied, open-hearted, tender merging of lips, of tongues. Breeeathe, staying open, feeling into their heart, gazing into their soul. Breathe in, feeling every nuance of sense and rush, and offer the flow of your experience as you breathe out. The smallest softening in the midst of this kiss becomes an invitation to more, surrendering even more into a deeper, wider, more energy-filled experience of receiving and offering the divinity of communion. Risk ravishment; risk swooning.

Practice Edgelessness

Even people who've developed an integrated awareness of body and mind, and have a lively sense of being inside their whole body, often feel encapsulated within their own bag of skin. To become one with another, to merge into a sense of *us,* those hard edges need to soften and lose their sense of self-definition. In an energetic sense it's necessary to climb into your beloved's skin and feel the heart that pulses with love.

1. Lie face to face with your partner, entwined as tightly as possible. Pressed this way, feel all the world that surrounds you, that cradles you, that pushes you together.

2. Lose the sense of where you end and your partner begins, and take this edgelessness into kisses with no edges.

3. After many minutes or hours of kissing, close your eyes and touch your foreheads together. Merge with everything that you discover there.

Lips only sing when they cannot kiss.

—James Thomson, 19th-century English poet

Telepathic Mail (T-mail)

As the two of you become more clearly One with each other, you will develop abilities that you may have noticed in other deep lovers. Not only will you begin to read each other's physical energy, but you will also recognize the flow of their emotions and begin to know their mind. Being able to finish each other's sentences is one sign that this is happening. Or the phone rings and it's the person you were just thinking of calling. Or you answer each other's questions before they are asked or as your letters are passing in the mail.

This connection is a reflection of the ways in which we are not separate but are woven into a web of communion. Whenever we are thinking about another, especially when combined with strong feelings, we are sending T-mail: telepathic messages that energetically telegraph themselves to the object of our attention. It's a wonderful way to share your bounty of love and kisses.

Have you read your T-mail? You have to be in a state of relaxation to receive subtle telepathic messages from other people, and that's rare for most folks. You may find that ideas and messages come to you best in the shower or when you're on a walk or doing mundane tasks like mowing the lawn. Your mind needs to be relaxed and open to receive them. You may be better at picking up messages from your infant children or your pets because you don't expect them to talk out loud. Make yourself available to receive the love that people are sending you by giving yourself moments of peaceful silence. This is also the best energetic frame for sending your own T–love notes.

Sending T-mail

Practice sending messages to your partner while both of you are in the same room, lounging about. You access more of your brain when playing than when you are strategically focused, so don't go about it too seriously. Begin with a simple message, say of your dog wagging her tail. Imagine her as if she was in front of you, and feel the emotions you would feel as her tail flips around in circles and she smiles her doggie grin at you. It's important to feel energy that is congruent with your image.

Gradually move farther and farther out of your partner's energy field and into other rooms, maintaining a playful, relaxed feeling. Be clear about who is sending and who is receiving. Open your heart to receive, relax your mind, and allow the messages to fall into your consciousness as if Harry Potter's owl had dropped them off.

Open me, river me, do what you will.

—*Roberta Werdinger, American writer*

Earthy Communion

In addition to communion with each other, another level of connection is essential to human beings: communion with the mother of us all, Mama Earth. Without a fundamental immersion in nature we will always feel homeless, and with it we always have a ground upon which to stand. Everything in our life springs from this relationship with the presence and energy of the earth; it's our original home.

If you have no sense of grounding within yourself, you'll waste a lot of energy trying to create it outside of yourself, and you may even try to ground through your partner. This is the basic dysfunction of codependency. Everyone needs their own roots if they are to grow. We plant our roots in the ground wherever we are Now, allowing us to weave our energy with the energy of Mother Nature. We cannot surrender ourselves in intimacy with any sense of safety unless we've cultivated a sense of being able to stand our own ground first.

Spend some time relaxing, breathing, and *becoming one* with nature, and then bring these essential energies of the Big Mama into your loving. You'll feel an expanded sense of belonging, and of the fullness of the earth's resources, as you cultivate a rich, safe, intimate relationship with this earthy life.

Elemental Kisses

The elements of nature are as inherently woven into our watery and earthy cells as they are into our environment. Joining with these elemental vibrations subtly reweaves us to the energetic fabric of Mother Nature. The kissing practices in the following pages are written in a poetic, metaphorical form and invite you into a voluptuous, sensual interpretation. Take your time, and feel into the qualities of water, earth, fire, and air.

The exercises can be done singly or as a sequence and are limited only by your imagination, your ability to commune, and your bliss tolerance. If you layer the elements, each into the other, your experience will be exponentially expanded. Allow yourself to be swept away by the energy and feelings the elements generate in you.

Kiss as If You Are Earth

Before lips, remember nature spirit
Move slowly the soft animal that is you
Look around and fall in love with your surroundings
Arrive, very here, very now
Primal
Lips full, presence of ripe desire
Savoring textures of tongue and tooth
Breath deep growling and moan
Vines of arm and leg encircling
Flesh heaving into hills and valleys
Sooo solidly meeting you
I rest in trust
And trusting, kiss you strong and deep

Kiss as If You Are Air

Wind knows its direction, even if we do not
It seeks fresh, expansive joy
Cool fingers breezing over warm neck valleys
Sweet enlivening
Breathe thin and full of mountain scent
Brilliantly lit with sun's sharp angle
Kisses clean, vibrant communications of what is real
Or infused with musk of river valley
Warm wind and heavy with earthy moisture
Lips full of sweet thick breath of passion

Kiss as If You Are Water

Feel the rhythm of the waves pulsing through your body
Capture the rhythm with your breath
Lips merge as rivers into ocean
Taste the salty depths of the sea
and the fresh sweetness of the mountain brook
Rock with swells
Surrender within the cycles of motion and rest
Sinking into the softly undulating depths
even as all this is happening, now,
Breath alive, deeply now, now
Flowing lip and tongue

Kiss as If You Are Fire

Cool fingers seek the warm silk of your hair
Face mask of frozen burdens begins to melt
Cells awake, tingling with yearning life
Eyes flash into yours, telegraphing penetrating presence
Breath sucks in deep as our lips quiver and spark, not quite
touching
Rushes of electricity dance my spine, I tremble with voltage
Tongues flicker
Fingers penetrate through muscle and bone
Energy pulses through the space between molecules
Kisses light hot

LESSON 4

Heavy Breathing

Every day you play with the light of the universe.

—*Pablo Neruda, Chilean poet*

Igniting the force

By the mid-1970s I had completed almost a decade of study and practice in Eastern spirituality and psychic healing: the eight limbs of yoga; ayurvedic, Buddhist, and Taoist practices; and the hands-on healing skills of Huna (Polynesian spiritual healing) and Therapeutic Touch. I'd studied with some remarkable people, and these practices were a major part of my life. And yet it wasn't until 1978 that the astonishing power of the breath fully dawned on me. Every practice I'd done had some element of attention to breath, but it never registered that the breath was the key to the whole practice. This very physical act connects us to the power of our inner spirit in profound ways.

How we breathe is the key to our whole experience of daily reality, as well as a path beyond, into an expanded reality. It soothes or invigorates us, heals and restores us. Our emotional range of experience will be determined by how caged our breath has become. The quality of our receiving and offering is shared in our breath. We intend creation into the world with our breath; it is the carrier of spirit and life force. The breath, spirit, and life force leave the body together as we depart this worldly experience. Breathing is one of the most significant elements of physical, emotional, mental, and spiritual well-being. And breathing is at the core of one's ability to experience passion.

There is a way of breathing that's a shame and a suffocation; and there is another way of expiring, a love breath, that lets you open infinitely.

—*Rumi, 13th-century Persian mystic (translated by Coleman Barks)*

The Love fires

Your breathing is intimately connected to your ability to experience and express love. A held breath keeps your energetic charge turned down and your emotions blocked in your body. The deeper you breathe, the easier it is to muster natural sexual energy. Deep breathing ignites your sexual fires. The fullness of breath cultivates charge and intensity, and engenders the opening of your heart; it's what passion feels like.

Culturally we are mostly upper-chest breathers. Stress of all kinds creates energy patterns that keep us physically "uptight" as well as mentally tense, and either emotionally agitated or depressed. These patterns are intimately connected to our experience of breathing.

Shallow breathing generated by physical or emotional tension locks you into an experience of feeling stuck, trapped, tired, blocked, or numb. Upper-chest breathing allows you less than one-third of your possible oxygen intake. Imagine how weak a fire you would start with so little oxygen. This lack of oxygen and the accumulated physical tension block the flow of vitality and nutrients into your body, and the exit of toxins from your body. Eventually you feel depleted, stressed out.

Shallow breathing keeps you cut off from your lower body and puts a damper on your sexual energy. These tension patterns greatly inhibit your ability to feel your body and the flow of emotion within it. If you are to cultivate the arts of loving, these breathing and tension patterns will need attention. In fact, *loving attention,* in and of itself, when drawn into your body or into your breathing, can ease many of your *tensions.* Opening either your constricted breathing pattern or your physical contraction will enhance your mental clarity, your emotional depth, and all your day's experiences. Imagine the impact of that upon your loving. *Mmmmm!*

Breathing exercises that allow you a deepening sense of relaxation while keeping you vibrantly present are profoundly healing. They can be very simple, but often we need to allow a bit of playfulness to happen, a surprise for the body-mind, a way to experience something ordinary in a new way.

Balloon Breathing

This is an excellent exercise to do as a couple. After work or before bed it can help you both release the burdens of the day, as well as charge and balance your energy. Take your partner's hand and lie down in a comfortable place, indoors or out, where you will not be disturbed for ten to twenty minutes.

1. Place a pillow under your knees and allow your spine to relax. Rest your arms at your sides with palms up. Begin by taking a few deep breaths and allowing your body to melt into the ground when you exhale. Let yourself sigh as you do so. Savor this sensation for several breaths. This helps release and ground you.

2. Now allow yourself to imagine that you are a big balloon, in the exact shape of you. And imagine that the Universe is blowing you up through your belly button.

3. Surrender your usual sense of yourself, and allow yourself to become the balloon. Feel your body lightly float up as you are inflated. In your mind's eye, the air comes in through your belly, blowing into your whole body,

plumping out your legs and arms, out to your fingertips. Notice how you deflate a bit when the air leaves: a soft sigh escapes. Continue for several minutes, cultivating the sensations of being the balloon, opened up by the breath of the Universe.

4. When you finish, gently release the image and bring your attention to your whole self. Really notice how you feel. Ease. Freedom. Lightness. Simply being. Sweetness. Peace. See if you can carry this state of being into your next moments, perhaps into your next hug and your next kiss. Two balloons, being breathed by the Universe—a bearable lightness of being.

I think he is going to kiss me. I wonder how I will breathe. He kisses me. His closeness must have an antihistamine effect, because, though we kiss for a long time, I am able to breathe.

—*Ellyn Bache, American writer*

The Old In and Out

People are often stronger either as inhalers or as exhalers. Those who inhale strongly are capable of building charge, also called chi or bioenergy, in the body. Sexually, this means that they can get excited, usually very quickly, and sometimes stay charged for long periods of time. If their exhalation is weak, however, they may lack the fullness of surrender to experience the rush and release of orgasmic energy overtaking their body-mind. Weak exhalers often demand a certain level of control that blocks the full release of tension and the deep experience of freedom.

When your exhalation is strong, you're more likely to be able to really let go and allow the energies of passion to run through you. However, if your inhalation is weak, your ability to charge your body will be weak. You may climax really quickly before much charge has been built because your body is a weak container for chi. Your rush and release will be quick, less intense, and usually limited to small areas of the body.

Cultivate the habit of being aware of your breathing. If you are a shallow breather, see what it takes for you to drop more deeply into your body and open to more charge. You'll eventually feel more powerful, less scared, and less tense. Your heart will feel more comfortable being open, and you may find you are more capable of receiving your heart's desires.

Breathing Tip

Fall in love with breathing. Use whatever sense you enjoy to cultivate a sensual relationship with your breath. If you're a tactile person who really appreciates touch or massage, then lie down, exaggerate your breathing, and feel the movement of muscle and bone, fluid and vapor, massaging your internal organs and easing your outer tensions. After a while you'll be able to do this as you wait in line or drive in traffic. *Aaahhhh!*

If you're a person who swoons at the scent of lilacs growing in your neighbor's yard or the whiff of cologne your partner leaves on their pillow, then you are particularly capable of developing the breath. Breathe deeply in life, anywhere, anytime, with curiosity. Cultivate the habit of savoring your inhalations, opening to all the subtle scents of this earthy garden.

The wise man breathes from the bottoms of his feet.

—Old Chinese saying

fire in the Heart Loves fire in the Belly

raditional Taoist sexual energy lore teaches that there is an area on your pelvic floor that, when stimulated, will greatly increase your sexual energy flow. Because the value of this increased energy is beyond measure, it's called "the million-dollar spot." You can contract, or stimulate with finger pressure, the pubo-coccygeal muscles, located between the genitals and the anus.

To most modern Western women, this area is known as the Kegel zone; many have been taught to contract their pelvic floor muscles several times a day to maintain the health of the reproductive and urinary organs. What is less well known is that this practice is also extremely useful for men; it increases both the vitality of the prostate gland and genital function.

By contracting and relaxing the pelvic floor muscles, you engage the energy of the root chakra, the energy center at the base of the spine. This cultivates a grounding effect for your bioelectricity, and as with any electrical circuitry, grounding allows energy to circulate freely through the body without shorting out.

Once you get your energy system grounded using Kegel contractions, extend your breath from the lower belly (or from your feet if you can) into the upper chest. The effects of this exercise are healing, potent, and immediate. Combining the pelvic floor muscle contraction with full lung breathing has the effect of energetically connecting the genitals and the heart as well as activating a robust energy charge. This breathing practice unites the energy of earthy sexuality with the energy of the Inner Lover in the spiritual energy body. The Inner Lover's essential vital forces are accessed in the heart's energy center, the heart chakra, located inside the body in the mid-chest. (For more on Kegel exercises, see Exercises 4.2a to 4.2c.)

Chakras and Subtle Energy Bodies

Energy fields in and around the body are a common element in visual art and in the writings of mystical cultures all over the world. One regularly seen image is that of a human with bright orbs of light radiating out from seven areas of their head and torso. In Eastern healing and tantric teachings, these centers are called "chakras." Each of these seven energy orbs in the body, from tailbone to head crown, serves as a communication system between the five energy grids that activate our body, mind, emotions, intuition, and spiritual inspiration. Each of these modes of perception has its own subtle energy field through which it sends information into the chakras. Each chakra has a different frequency and relates to correlated parts of the body and psyche. Information from your inner self is telegraphed to your body through the appropriate chakras.

What we feel and think has an immediate impact on the processes of our body. Every time we think or feel anything, the message vibrates electrically in our energy field and is registered in our body. When, for instance, you feel excited, the chakras pulse and spin, sending energy to the physical body's energy meridians (the same ones the acupuncturists use), and on into the body tissues via the nerves. This electricity ignites chemical processes that the body uses to activate a response appropriate to the subtle messages from your inner self. Within a nanosecond you can feel excited, because your entire body is being flooded with hormones sending messages of excitation, all thanks to your chakras.

When our energy system is working well, we experience ourselves as feeling grounded in the Here, centered in the Now, sensually alive, freely creative, highly capable in the world, able to feel a wide range of emotions, thinking clearly and easily, and open to inspiration. Our energy system is the link in the body-mind-spirit matrix.

Most everyone would benefit from knowing how to intentionally activate and integrate their energy system, for we can all learn to be more powerful, open-hearted, and vital than we are now. The cultivation of a highly functioning energy system is intimately tied to our ability to open our heart and experience heightened states of passion, as well as to cultivate deep, expansive states of consciousness and vibrant health. Energy integration and cultivation is an essential and fundamental teaching in traditional sexual energy practices like Tibetan tantra, Taoist sexual kung fu, and the shamanic magical arts of sexual energy.

Introduction to Chakra functions

Each chakra plays a particular role in the makeup of our inner experience and in the functions of the body. These centers of energetic integration and communication are usually numbered, beginning at the base of the torso, up through the middle of the body, and on to the crown of the head. The vibrational speed and efficiency of these energy centers are vitally connected to the fullness of our breath, our ability to be fully present in the body, and our willingness to experience the depth and richness of our inner self.

When fully opened and functioning, the chakras are round globes inside the body that may swell to the size of a honeydew melon, or occasionally even larger. Some ascribe the colors of the rainbow to the chakras, while others see a complex and unique palette when psychically viewing these energy centers.

Chakra 1: The base or root chakra is located at the base of the body, around the tailbone. This is the energetic root that grounds our bioelectrical energy fields to the earth. Humans have a complex bioelectrical energy system, and like any electrical system, our energy will short out if we're not grounded. Our first chakra vibrates with the attitudes we hold, and the habits we cultivate, in *relationship to the earth.* Do you feel that you are a guest on the earth or that you're connected to the life force of the trees, weather, soil, and animals? Do you feel that you have to struggle to survive or that the earth is an abundant place? These beliefs will cultivate a particular energetic relationship with the parts of your body around this energy center. A healthy root chakra will bring us the strength to stand our ground, providing the anchoring that allows us to manifest our dreams.

Chakra 2: The second chakra is located in the pelvis and is the energy center in charge of our *sexual and creative energy*. This chakra is also in charge of all manner of *flow* in our entire system: flow of energy, fluids, thoughts, feelings, inspiration, manifestation. A healthy sex-and-creativity chakra opens us to the flow of warmth and sensuality found in our sexual energy. This flow adds grace and fullness to our presence and a luxurious quality to our loving. Creativity is also opened when we are running our sexual energy, and flows into a rush of inspiration and fresh perspectives. Both orgasms and creativity are accessed at the edges of our personality; both require a deep surrender in order to explode into another octave of Being.

Chakra 3: Often called the solar plexus chakra, the third chakra is the communication center of our *personal power*. Do you feel you can cope? That you are capable? Deserving? Of value? That you can, and you will? What is your relationship with the world? Can you share? Are people created equal? To whom do you give your power?

Chakra 4: The heart chakra, located in the center of the chest, is one of the larger chakras and contains several functions. The chakra itself is the communication center of warmth, sweetness, and acceptance. Here we have compassion for ourselves and for others. This chakra is in charge of *receiving*. Is your heart-receiver open or closed? Also found within this energy center is the soul, the emotionally coded memory of all our experiences from all "time." Our soul records our life from the emotions we are experiencing; these are our memories. The spiritual energy body itself resides within everyone's heart chakra as well. This is the source of energy that runs our entire system. The more we connect with this, our richest energy resource, the more potent our life force becomes, and the more connected we feel to all of life. In people whom we think of as mystics or saints, this spiritual energy field expands to fill their entire body. Their experience is that *all is spirit.*

Chakra 5: The throat chakra, located from the collarbone to the jaw hinge, is in charge of *you being received.* This is the center of wisdom, of being deeply heard, both internally and externally. It is where we speak our truth, or get choked up and don't. We experience a lot of neck and jaw tension when we block the expression of our truth.

Chakra 6: The sixth chakra is sometimes called the third-eye chakra. We have two eyes that look out into the world and one that looks within. This is the center of intuition, insight, imagination, and psychic knowing. In actuality, it is not a true chakra but an energy body in itself. When fully functioning, as in mystics and those with extrasensory perception, the *psychic energy body* expands to fill the entire physical body.

Chakra 7: The crown chakra is quite large when fully open and is seen extending from the jaw hinge to several inches over the head. This energy center is connected to our deepest inner resources, the *mind of God.* It is our access to what is called "the higher power" or "the higher Self," and is the nimbus seen in paintings around the heads of saints and deities.

Beginning Kegel Breathing

Kegel breathing draws energy away from the overactive mind, gets you more fully into your body, and fires up the electrical circuits that conduct your life force. This practice can cultivate a profound potency of energy within an astonishingly peaceful sense of wholeness. This is the perfect time to share intimately with your partner, for you are intimately connected with yourself. Feel yourself breathing with your whole body as you kiss your beloved from toe to nose. A divine experience!

1. Place your awareness on the pelvic floor, the area of the root chakra, locating the pubo-coccygeal muscles.

2. Contract these muscles, lifting them like an elevator toward your head.

3. As you hold the Kegel contraction, *inhale* from as deep in the body as possible, pulling the breath up into the upper chest.

4. *Exhale,* releasing the contraction and feeling your energy flood into your lower torso and legs.

Kegel/Heart Breathing

1. Proceed as in beginning Kegel breathing (Exercise 4.2a), and while *inhaling,* bring the breath up to the heart chakra located in the mid-chest.

2. *Open* the heart chakra wide (it can grow to about the size of a volleyball) and let it instantly fill with light, as if you'd suddenly opened a camera lens.

3. You are actually opening the spiritual energy body here in your heart; *feel into the sweetness and vitality* of your most potent inner resource.

4. *Exhale,* sending this light down into the lower torso while releasing the Kegel contraction.

Grounded Kegel/Heart Breathing

1. Proceed as in Exercises 4.2a and 4.2b. With your exhalation send the heart chakra light *down* the torso and continue down from the feet, imagining yourself growing healthy strong tree roots from the feet, which flow down into the earth.

2. Continue the Kegel contraction and release, inhaling fully up into your chest and exhaling the light from your heart chakra down into your roots for several breaths, feeling into the experience.

3. When a strong energetic ground is formed, you will probably notice tingling in your feet and/or the root chakra near the base of your spine. You may also sense the strong flow of energy circulating through your body's meridian system, as well as feeling stronger and heavier, more solid and potent.

The kisses, which bring me back to life . . .

—George Sand, 19th-century French writer

Breathing as a Couple

Breathing together intentionally is a lovely way to harmonize energetically with your partner and to get vitality flowing in your bodies. These exercises are basic to many sacred sexual traditions. Practice both the synchronized pattern and the oppositional pattern, together or at separate times. The first breath practice gets you both on the same page, and the second is like partner dancing and kissing, where juicy energy is exchanged. Both cultivate intimacy, a willingness to be seen, felt, and received.

Harmony Breathing

1. Take your partner by the hand and bring them to a quiet place where you can settle comfortably for several minutes. Your intention is to become fully present and harmonious with your beloved.

2. Sit in front of each other and softly gaze into each other's left eye. As discussed in the previous chapter, the left eye nurtures feminine energy, so this gaze builds connection.

3. One of you is chosen to start and begins to breathe sensuously and deeply.

4. The second partner joins in and matches the breathing pattern. Continue for several minutes. *You may end the practice here or continue with a deepening practice.*

5. After several minutes in real harmony, the first partner gets up and begins slowly walking around.

6. The second partner follows, continuing to match the

first partner's breathing pattern. Continue for several minutes; then switch who is leading and following, changing your roles.

7. Share with your beloved what occurred for you.

Breathing Tips

Many wonderful books and tapes with breathing practices are available these days. Enjoy them, play with the practices, and explore your potential for creating a fully charged life force and a very potent love force.

At least once a day, take a breather. Just focus on breathing the way you do when you are experiencing pleasure.

Oppositional Breathing for Couples

Your intention in this practice is to deepen your energetic rapport with your partner and share some energy. The emotional tone you carry will flavor the exchange. I would encourage having a little fun.

1. Gather yourself and your partner into a comfortable place and sit in front of each other, knees touching.

2. Gaze into each other's left eye and relax, or maybe flirt a little.

3. Choose which of you will start (Partner A) and which will follow (Partner B). Partner A should begin breathing, exaggerating the breathing a little so it is easy for Partner B to feel the rhythm.

4. Partner B should then begin to inhale as Partner A is exhaling, breathing in their energy.

5. Partner B then exhales, and Partner A inhales B's exhalation and energy. This rhythm takes a minute to settle into. Stay very present, feeling the rhythm of in and out, of sharing each other's life force.

6. Continue for ten minutes or more.

LESSON 5

Express Yourself

The only gift is a portion of thyself.

—Ralph Waldo Emerson, 19th-century American essayist and poet

Show Some Emotion

Nothing is worse than a dead-fish kiss: cold, flat, communicating nothing more than a sense of duty or obligation. That's a sure path away from intimacy and into the land of hurt and resentment. Don't be afraid to open up and let pleasure and satisfaction be expressed when you are nuzzling, necking, and making out. Groans, moans, and other expressions of delight tell your partner that you are truly enjoying your kissing experience. Emotional feedback is the most evocative form of communication, getting our attention by animating the physical body.

Emotions have power and impact. A surrendered sigh that shudders up from our depths is a breath that has been waiting, *yearning to exhale,* and it can melt a timid heart. A shiver that rushes down the body and curls your toes is clearly a moving experience, a flood of potent energies moving you, and a clear communication to your partner that you are experiencing something powerful. When we open to a full range of emotions, the entire body becomes a conduit for the flow of the energy that gets triggered by our body's hormonal system. This is chemistry in action. This is what gives a kiss its ability to transform us.

Clearly, emotional freedom is not something we experience often in our head-driven culture. Ever wonder why the lovers in the hotter movies amplify their moans and love cries? It's so the audience will have no doubt about what is evolving and where the actors stand on the "Oh *yes!*" or "I'm coming!" scale.

It's an art to be finely tuned in and to experience emotional subtlety in ourselves and others. Many times folks don't know if the sound their partner is making means that they are swooning with delight or about to cough. Most lovers are not schooled in the arts of emotional expression and can't read hints very well, so they relate more to the volume of communication than to nuances. It's the *emotion in the sound, rather than the decibels,* that conveys the message with a visceral impact.

Emotional expression grounds us in our experience as it's happening, and cultivates embodied intimacy. When we clearly sense the feelings of our partner, we can relax our pressure to perform and simply engage in the sharing of feelings through the teasing, hungering, lingering, frenetic, tender, succulent, and oh-sooo-responsive kiss.

A kiss can be a comma, a question mark or an exclamation point.

—*Mistinguett, 19th-century French entertainer*

Cultivating a Language of Emotion

The immediacy of our emotions often gets lost in our attempts to talk about them, for we've gone to the head to find the language of the body, perhaps days after the experience. And so we end up with a lot of emotional residue instead of the direct experience of the moment. Getting this backlog dumped on us is a sure way to block intimacy and feel the burden of emotional repression.

To cultivate immediacy and fluidity in your emotional exchanges with your partner, *make an agreement to speak in gibberish when in the midst of an emotional encounter.* For instance, if you're being stirred by anger and fear, wanting to rant, then belt it out. It could sound something like *"Gibberan tate! Dabubu waaba nuffet!"* Any sounds that come to you are the right ones as long as there are no recognizable words, no matter what the language. This way there will be no charged words that hurt later on; your partner won't be able to take them personally. You won't need to beat yourself up over what you said in a not so pretty moment, nor will your beloved store up your words for further ammunition at a later date. It doesn't matter what the "words" end up being; go for the emotional tone that expresses the energy rushing through you.

Cultivate a full range of emotions. Practice talking gibberish in the shower or alone in the car, so you can be spontaneous in the moment of sharing. A softer moment might include cooing sounds: *"Nanaa buuufo abada, dedediwa. Naa?"* Or a tease in public can be offered without others knowing: *"Danna wabo, yta ba. Bubabam yata namba?"* If the energy of the emotion is carried through your voice and tone and body language, the odds are good that your partner will know just what you mean. If they don't, then feel even more deeply and invite the anguish of not being heard and felt to flow through your next gibberish communiqué.

Her lips on his could tell him better than all her stumbling words.

—Gone with the Wind, *by Margaret Mitchell, American writer*

Set Yourself Free

Remember that physical tensions are huge blocks to emotional expression. Any tensions in the torso will block energy from filling that part of our body, which means that we will be walled off from part of our body's physical and emotional experience.

Blocking charge in the pelvis is a common practice, and it greatly affects our experience of intimacy. This is accomplished by locking the lower back, not swinging our hips, and taking shallow breaths.

Most of us habitually control the amount of energy we send to our pelvis because our puritanical culture has taught us to limit our experience of our "lower" body in favor of "being nice." We block the energy in order to feel that we're in control of just how much energy, and what kind of energy, we are willing to share. Over time we lose much of that control, however, and simply become habituated to not feeling our body and the emotions that flow through it.

The locked lower body blocks the free movement of the diaphragm, which in turn limits our breath to the upper chest. Breathing shallowly keeps our experience tense, our passion shallow, and our communication halfhearted. Feeling is blocked, sexual energy is blocked, our charge is limited, and our head is mentally and emotionally disconnected from our body. From this stance it's almost impossible to even know what we feel, much less how to express it. These disconnections generate experiences of low-level intimacy, frustration, and boredom—all spawning lots of reasons not to kiss, not to feel, not to connect.

The neighbors are hearing when you fight and argue; why not let them know you also make love?

—Osho, Indian mystic

Risk Letting Go

Interestingly, the energy centers that animate our sexual energy, personal power, and sense of physical safety are all in the lower half of the torso. We're usually aching for the experience of this deeper, more grounded connection with ourselves because it is so often locked away. The full-body breath is one key to opening these vital energy centers; another is the freedom to express emotions and allow them to move through the whole body. This expanded flow of feeling, breath, and expression is as important to a deep kiss as it is to deep orgasm, vibrant health, and deep love.

If you want rushes of feeling to thrill and engorge you, you will need to intentionally share potent emotion in an open, relaxed body. A tensely held body, an armored chest protecting a fearful heart, or a stiff upper lip will not allow subtle emotional energy to rush through. For this energy to transmute the daily grind into a magical merging of lip and tongue, we need a willingness to open, a willingness to be physically rocked by the tunes our hearts are playing. That shuddering sigh that rushes to exhale heralds a deeper willingness to risk moving into the unknown flows of our full self. This is where we can offer our deepest, most surrendered, potent kiss.

Give yourself permission to let go and surrender, melting the walls of tension both within you and between your partner. Soften, slow down, and offer tenderness, purring, nuzzling—the sounds of sweet letting go. Your breathy sounds, twitching lips, and emotional energy are vibrations in motion, the electrical force behind your chemistry.

This morning I wished (once) to be a quiet
lover, but who can love with a closed mouth?

—Elizabeth Alexander, American poet

Sighing Practice

Our culture tends to assume that when someone is sighing, they are bored or maybe disgusted. Why do people never assume that the person is relaxing? The sigh is a powerful signal to our nervous system to let go. Think of sinking into a big, wonderful bath with the water at your favorite temperature, and just the right soap, and your favorite number of candles. Settle in, relax, and allow yourself to lie weightless and surrendered. Take a very deep breath, open the back of your throat, and *sssiiiiiigh. Aaahhhhh.* Cultivate this activity of surrender and bring it into your snuggling, and kissing, and wordless conversations.

Sighing 101

Lie back wherever you can and take a few very deep breaths, stretching open your belly and chest. Count as you inhale, and double that count as you let your air out, making your exhalation twice as long as your inhalation. Open up the back of your throat. Exhale and let a sigh come from as deep in your body as you can. *Aaaahhhhh . . .*

You may feel really tight in your throat and only squeak at first. Just keep dropping into deeper states of relaxation as you continue to melt with the long, deep sigh. You may also need to suspend those beliefs about how nice people don't make noises. *Aaaahhhhh,* do it in the tub, do it when you lie down, do it in the traffic jam or between projects; sigh and sigh again. Feel your nervous system relax, your breathing expand, your voice become resonant, and your mind lighten up.

Energetically you're opening up the throat chakra and releasing the overcharged energy in your head, allowing it to rush into the lower chakras and generate physical vitality.

Every night, we nestle like ducks in bed, sharing intimate whispers,
our bodies become at one.

—*Ikkyu Sojun, 15th-century Zen master*

Pillow Talk

illow talk is the language of lovers, the conversations we share in private moments about our intimate experience. Many people do not speak in this lovers' language at all, fearing that what would be said at such times might be too racy or wounding, or simply poorly received. This is a great loss, for it's in these moments that we most often have our guard down, which is when the possibility of real intimacy is near.

Try speaking of what is most precious in these moments: the sweetness of your beloved's caress, the moment you felt them merge right through your skin into your heart. Speak of the feeling that rushed through you as their eyes opened suddenly, piercingly, and looked so deeply into you. Share the feeling of peace and safety you feel as you lie in their arms. Be a grateful lover, appreciating, praising, and enjoying.

If, however, you were less than thrilled by the caress or merge, then speak of the gifts you yearn to share: your longing, your desires, your eagerness to go deeper, to learn to love more fully. Risk a deeper conversation, a sharing at the edge of your growth.

We live in emotionally repressive times, and we have a lot of resistance to letting go and allowing ourselves to be emotionally vulnerable and open; but regardless of kissing technique, it's just not possible to have toe-curling experiences of passion transmitted through us if we, or our partner, are mentally, emotionally, or physically "shut down." Our systems will not be resonant enough to carry the necessary electricity for passion. The difference between the energetic frequency of a closed emotion, such as guilt or shame, and an open emotional flow, such as full-on acceptance, is like the difference between a 15-watt and a 250-watt lightbulb. We weaken our energy systems when we habitually run weak emotional energy flows, and our kisses and lovemaking will reflect that difference. If you want thrilling kisses, you're going to have to be willing to get out of your head, relax your body, open your heart, breathe deeply, and let the emotions rip! There is no other way to cultivate bliss.

How to Say "I Love You" in 100 Languages

Afrikaan: Ek het jou life

Albanian: Te dua

Arabic: Ana behibak (to male), Ana behibek (to female)

Armenian: Yes kez sirumen

Bambara: M'bi fe

Bangla: Aamee tuma ke bhalo aashi

Belarusian: Ya tabe kahayu

Bisaya: Nahigugma ako kanimo

Bulgarian: Obicham te

Cambodian: Soro lahn nhee ah

Cantonese Chinese: Ngo oiy ney a

Catalan: T'estimo

Cheyenne: Ne mohotatse

Chichewa: Ndimakukonda

Corsican: Ti tengu caru (to male), Ti tengu cara

Creole: Mi aime jou

Croatian: Volim te

Czech: Miluji te

Danish: Jeg Elsker Dig

Dutch: Ik hou van jou

English: I love you

Esperanto: Mi amas vin

Estonian: Ma armastan sind

Ethiopian: Afgreki'

Faroese: Eg elski teg

Farsi: Doset daram

Filipino: Mahal kita

Finnish: Mina rakastan sinua

French: Je t'aime, Je t'adore

Frisian: Ik hâld fan dy

Gaelic: Ta gra agam ort

Georgian: Mikvarhar

German: Ich liebe dich

Greek: S'agapo

Gujarati: Hoo thunay prem karoo choo

Hawaiian: Aloha Au Ia`oe

Hebrew: Ani ohev otah (to female), Ani ohev et otha (to male)

Hiligaynon: Guina higugma ko ikaw, Palangga ko ikaw

Hindi: Hum Tumhe Pyar Karte hae

Hmong: Kuv hlub koj

Hopi: Nu' umi unangwa'ta

Hungarian: Szeretlek

Icelandic: Eg elska tig

Ilonggo: Palangga ko ikaw

Indonesian: Saya cinta padamu

Inuit: Negligevapse

Irish: Taim i' ngra leat

Italian: Ti amo

Japanese: Aishiteru

Kannada: Naanu ninna preetisuttene

Kapampangan: Kaluguran daka

Kiswahili: Nakupenda

Konkani: Tu magel moga cho

Korean: Sarang Heyo

Latin: Te amo

Latvian: Es tevi miilu

Lebanese: Bahibak

Lithuanian: Tave myliu

Malay: Saya cintakan mu, Aku cinta padamu

Malayalam: Njan Ninne Premikunnu

Mandarin Chinese: Wo ai ni

Marathi: Me tula prem karto

Mohawk: Kanbhik

Moroccan: Ana moajaba bik

Nahuatl: Ni mits neki

Navaho (Dineh): Ayor anosh'ni

Norwegian: Jeg Elsker Deg

Pandacan: Syota na kita!!

Pangasinan: Inaru Taka

Papiamento: Mi ta stimabo

Persian: Doo-set daaram

Pig Latin: Iay ovlay ouyay

Polish: Kocham Ciebie

Portuguese: Eu te amo

Romanian: Te iubesc

Russian: Ya tebya liubliu

Scot Gaelic: Tha gradh agam ort

Serbian: Volim te

Setswana: Ke a go rata

Sign Language: ,\,,/ (represents position of fingers when signing "I love you")

Sindhi: Maa tokhe pyar kendo ahyan

Sioux: Techihhila

Slovak: Lu`bim ta

Slovenian: Ljubim te

Spanish: Te quiero, Te amo

Surinam: Mi lobi joe

Swahili: Ninapenda wewe

Swedish: Jag alskar dig

Swiss-German: Ich lieb Di

Tagalog: Mahal kita

Tahitian: Ua Here Vau Ia Oe

Taiwanese: Wa ga ei li

Tamil: Nan unnai kathalikaraen

Telugu: Nenu ninnu premistunnanu

Thai: Chan rak khun (to male), Phom rak khun (to female)

Turkish: Seni Seviyorum

Ukrainian: Ya tebe kahayu

Urdu: Mai aap say pyaar karta hoo

Vietnamese: Anh ye^u em (to female), Em ye^u anh (to male)

Welsh: 'Rwy'n dy garu di

Yiddish: Ikh hob dikh

Yoruba: Mo ni fe

LESSON 6

Got Rhythm?

If I were what the words are,
And love were like the tune,
With double sound and single
Delight our lips would mingle,
With kisses glad as birds are
That get sweet rain at noon.

—*Algernon Swinburne, 19th-century English poet*

Getting into the Groove

New experiences grab our attention. When we learn to drive a car, we're paying attention to every nuance of road curves, traffic flows, foot pedals, gear sticks, music controls, heating knobs, and speed gauges. It's a lot to hold in our awareness, and it takes some getting used to. Sooner or later we get the rhythm in our body, and from then on we barely notice anything about the driving experience. We automatically do the dance of clutch and gear, signal and turn.

Imagine that you're driving along, thinking about dinner or eating an apple. You're not even glancing down at the control panel unless something unusual starts blinking. As far as driving goes, you're on automatic pilot.

The level of mastery that you've achieved by training yourself to drive effortlessly offers you two choices of attention. The easier choice is to allow the autopilot to run the driving experience, and to let your mind leave your body and float off somewhere else. This is when you find yourself trailing along a stream of thoughts that have nothing to do with driving. I would guess that most people are driving in this mode.

A deeper choice is to bring your mind fully back into your body and expand your attention in the midst of your effortless driving. You're attending to all the nuances of driving with part of your awareness, while opening your mind even more deeply into what else is occurring in this moment. Being more fully Here, Now, in your body, in the weather, in the music, in your heart, in your toes.

You notice that you'd been driving in a flatland while out of body, and now the scenery is exquisitely 3-D. Colors are brighter; you can feel the motion of the clouds as they race across the sky. You're intuitively connected to the driving patterns of the cars around you and can sense what their intentions are, and you dance gracefully around them. You feel the music playing on the radio and your body moves a little to the groove, to the emotion. You're fully present, open, and not muting out your experience but savoring it. There is a natural sense of order and pulse to life all around you, and you are intimately connected to it. In the midst of this fullness of presence, the most amazing inspirations can occur, for you are not resisting anything. You are in direct and open relationship with *what is*.

When you choose to be fully present and open in loving, the quality of your experience will always be fresh. It will always be new, because you are in this new moment experiencing *what is*. And *what is* is always changing. The various rhythms of these changing moments generate the pulse we can groove to in kissing, in relating, in sexing, in all of life. Our choice in every minute is either to pull out of our experience or to dive into it, to resist or to find the rhythm.

Kiss after kiss without cessation

Until we lose all calculation.

—*Catullus, Roman poet, 1st century B.C.*

The Dance of the Kiss fantastic

L istening, moving, and kissing to the dance and the music of love, relish this moment of Now, this luscious *what is.* Feel the rhythm of give-and-take as the energy of intimacy weaves your separate Nows together.

If you're open to *what is,* you will notice that every moment has an emotional quality. This is more evident when the moment is shared with the intimate other, because we reflect and bounce emotional energy off each other. This emotional play is one of the primary drives of a relationship. We get really high from this emotional give-and-take because it builds rapport, it's what hot intimacy feels like. We swap energy back and forth, which builds passionate charge and loving depth and an exhilarating expansion of experience.

Your partner shuts down with your kiss, and quickly you call upon your Inner Lover, feel your heart, and hear the message "Lighten up!" You respond, and something new develops. You pick up your beloved's hand and kiss it as if you've found just what you're looking for. Appreciation is a powerful heart opener. You learn to never go further until you're both feeling at least a little open-hearted.

The most tuned-in kissers recognize that these emotional energy exchanges have a rhythmic quality to them that can wondrously choreograph our kissing moments. These qualities can be felt or read just like any piece of music. Are we playing the blues tonight, my love? *Feeeel* into the vibe between you, and be curious.

Sense the physical stirrings of your own body. Where in your body do you feel alive? Where are you numb? Are you tight, tired? Do you feel shallow, timid, hungry, abandoned? Or is there a radiance, a tangible presence in you that feels so alive that it vibrates right through your skin? How are you breathing? Where is it stuck? How open is the flow of energy in your body? Is it hot or cold? Have these physical sensations changed since you started paying attention to them?

Now come together and begin to feel into each other's body. Tune in to the pulsing of your hearts; are you flowing languidly into a sultry waltz? There are complex kissing rhythms that play like French bistro music, mixing a jazzy ethnic charge into the dance of lips, the flick of tongue, the capture of one lip. Here we find more moans, deep breathing, hungry arms, greedy lips, and teasing play of eye. Or is it that buckle-polishing Cajun tempo that has you throbbing? Bring your breathy, nostril-flaring energy into your kissing.

When Dysrhythmia Happens

In any relationship, your rhythms are sometimes out of synch with your partner's. You're up, they're down. You're stressed, and they want to take the kids to the circus. In cardiology lingo, if your heart's rhythm is chaotic you are said to be suffering from *dysrhythmia*. When we're confused or distressed, we experience a chaotic disturbance of heart and mind within ourselves, and we bring our dysrhythmia into our relationships. These are times when we can either head off in different directions, guarding our separation, or choose to meet on a new level, to develop intimacy. This is when the Inner Lover takes out the toolbox and chooses the practices that will artfully reshape the energy between you and your beloved.

Consider, are you feeling stressed out and spun up? That's a really good time to take a walk together and do some deep breathing, or trade massages; perhaps a head, neck, and shoulder session or a foot rub sounds good. Are you feeling emotionally distant, isolated? Try some left-eye gazing with your partner while you breathe in the same rhythm. Or, if you can't see eye to eye, perhaps you need to stay in your mood and try to work it out by dancing back to back (see Exercise 6.1).

Dancing Back to Back

When we're in a different energetic rhythm than our partner but still really wanting to connect with them, it's best to let our bodies do the talking. If a walk isn't sounding like fun, then take ten minutes and crank up the body language by getting more rigorously engaged with each other, back to back and booty to booty.

1. Put on some music with a strong rhythm, and turn it up loud.

2. Take off your shoes and socks so you can feel your feet and stand your ground.

3. Lean into each other, back to back, and boogie down to your own mood, as your partner will to theirs.

4. Make whatever sound your body wants to release.

5. Keep dancing back to back for ten to twenty minutes, feeling each other's emotions through the body. Try leaning into your partner, or supporting them as they lean into you. Notice who demands control, or how you're handing over your own control.

6. After a while you may notice that you and your partner have grown more closely aligned in your movement, rhythm, and groove. You may also notice that you just got a great workout on top of a back massage. Turn face to face, hug, and climb into each other's heart.

7. Caress each other's face and let those lips have the next dance.

It was a strange sensation, a clumsy stumbling falling being caught,
the broad sunlit world narrowing to the dark focus of his cushiony
lips on mine. It scared me to death, but still I discovered how much
I had been waiting for it.

——A Thousand Acres, *by Jane Smiley, American writer*

Communicating Rhythm

All types of partner dancing include practices for cultivating the passionate art of sharing feminine and masculine energy, and these principles also apply to the dance of intimacy between partners. One of the basic lessons in most forms of hands-on dancing is that both partners have to hold a bit of strength in their arms and torso so that the communication from leader to follower can be telegraphed through the bones and muscles and nerves. This is called *holding the frame.* You're not stiff, but strongly present, alive and responsive.

The partner holding the masculine energy leads the dance. Masculine energy, by nature and biology, is penetrating and directing, and has a palpable animal presence to it. This vibe of masculine presence and claim is often what is most sexy to people with a feminine sexual essence.

If the masculine partner's energy is weak, his "frame" will be flabby and his energy will not be able to penetrate and lead the feminine. If he's lost in thought, his energy will be scattered and he will be unable to lead clearly. She, and the dance, will inevitably suffer in some way from his lack of connection and direction. As a result, she may decide to activate her own masculine energy and begin controlling them both.

Or, feeling unmet and hurt, she may decide not to play at all and either shut down, pull away, or disconnect from her body and emotions. She has not been met, and trust has been lost.

Weak masculine energy in loving and kissing means a lack of ravishment, presence, and claim. The results are tepid, distant, dutiful, or deadened kisses. *Blech!* A communication of lack and a lack of communication. What is communicated is this: "I lack the skills for holding presence, or the ability to connect with myself. I lack the depth of feeling, power, and charge that generates chemistry."

Similarly, if the partner holding the feminine energy is not charged enough to "hold the frame" in the partner dance of waltzing, or making whoopee, she won't be able to receive the masculine partner's leading guidance. The message telegraphed through him won't find the presence necessary to receive and respond to the message. It'll be like trying to push a piece of rope; the frame will collapse.

Weak feminine energy stays cool; it doesn't charge up and carry heat. In kissing, this means a lack of response, a sloppiness in the rhythm, a give-and-take that never gets going. There may well be a holding on, a resistance to opening, to feeling, to breathing and sharing. There is lack of trust in the safety and flow of feminine surrender.

Rhythm Practice

Without working yourself into a frenzy, exchange a series of slow, meaningful kisses. Cultivate a rhythm in your kissing and breath, becoming totally in tune with one another, as though you're in a tango-style dance. This creates sensual energy, connecting you to your body-mind. Pacing is important; to surrender our defenses, we need to feel safe and cherished. One partner may lead this dance of lip and tongue, or you may play back and forth, switching every few seconds depending on the tempo of the encounter.

Kissing is a dance, maybe a slow dance at first, feeling into each other, connecting. Sense the lead and surrender, and follow along as the tempo increases, as breath quickens. This feeds the negative-positive charge of your sexual energies. Incorporate flirting and playfulness; vary the pressure, the embrace, the opening of eyes, the conversation that tongues can have.

Stay in present time. An unsyncopated rhythm means you're not connected, perhaps second-guessing your moves or racing toward some goal. Bring your attention back, and feel into your heart and find your beloved there. Gaze back into their eyes and adore them with abandon. Kiss your partner with this feeling rushing through you, and be there for whatever magic happens next.

Dance

I was convinced I couldn't dance. Then I met a man who patiently taught me to dance a little. He made it fun, had a great sense of humor about it. The first time we danced in public I was so happy. We knew two steps, and we were just doing the same things over and over, but I was so giddy I was dizzy with it. I could only dance with a person I knew well. How can you follow a stranger, how can you possibly predict what he's about to do? I need to be able to read every little gesture and expression. It's such an intimate thing, following somebody's lead. We stare coldly into each other's eyes and waltz in these mad centrifugal circles exactly like we were one person. My face goes into his chest at exactly the right place. I have to go into a kind of trance to be able to follow him. If you think about it you'll stumble and mess up and step all over his feet. I used to try to count in my head. But now I've figured out this trance deal where my face is in his chest and it's the twilight zone, time has stopped, the moment lasts forever. I could die right there, my ears ringing with joy.

—*Elizabeth Churchill, American writer*

LESSON 7

Do It Now

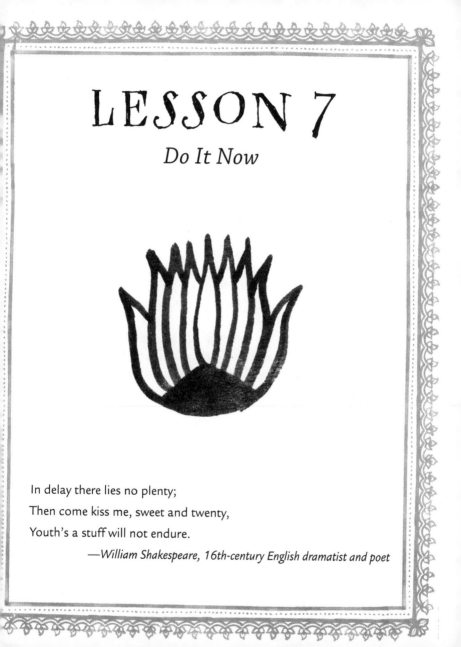

In delay there lies no plenty;

Then come kiss me, sweet and twenty,

Youth's a stuff will not endure.

—William Shakespeare, 16th-century English dramatist and poet

Got Jam?

Why do we wait until some other time to really, really, really share ourselves? I've never understood that. Some part of us believes that somehow loving, and much of living, will be better done in some other moment. That the better time to really live our life is when we are somehow more available, like when the job is going smoothly, when the kids are grown, after dinner, when the house is paid off, or when we're on vacation. I'm too busy for more than superficial loving, so not now, honey . . . *peck, peck.*

I'm reminded of an old nursery rhyme that says, "Jam tomorrow, and jam yesterday, but *never* jam today." How can there be jam tomorrow or even jam yesterday if there is never jam today? It's always today. This today, this moment, is the only moment we ever have to share what we feel. Bring on the jam!

Imagine that you are eating the last existing spoonful of your favorite ice cream, the last one in existence for all time; how would you be experiencing it? Would you wait to taste it, maybe save it for when you have more time and it has freezer burn? Would you gobble it, just getting it over with so you could mourn its loss? Or would you really taste it—all the nuances of creamy sweetness, all that extra-yummy flavor? How about smelling it, with real presence; inhaling intimately, gathering all the subtle scents that are writing notes on the pages of your memory? Are you letting it luxuriate in your mouth, stretching out the moment, loath to end this bliss? Go ahead, don't be shy when you notice you're making sounds of yumminess: oh yeah, mouth ecstasy!

Can you imagine sharing all this cherishing in your first kiss of the day? How would the deep, rich enjoyment of your lips, heart, scent, and feeling change your day? Oh, can we do it again at the first kiss upon arriving home? or in parting? or in the middle of making dinner? Why would I want anything less?

Gamble everything for love,

if you're a true human being.

—Rumi, 13th-century Persian mystic

feeeelings first

In an intimate conversation we respond primarily to the feeling of the message; the message itself is secondary. This is why a kiss that is empty of heart hurts so. Our memories are also encoded on the emotion of the experience. Two children from the same family have very different memories because they had different emotional responses to what they experienced. So this means that emotions are our first response and also the aspect of the experience that we take with us.

We seem to be afraid of real feelings these headstrong days; they're messy, not easily kept under control. People feel as though they are victims of their emotions, when in fact the deeper Self, who you really are, is far more powerful than the surface shift of mood and rush, and deeper still than the mind that is wanting to control all the flux of feeling. We create emotional habits and then identify with them: I am depressed, I am unlucky, I am a lousy lover. These are emotional patterns that become automatic, and then our experience is no longer fresh but simply a rerun of last season's programming.

You will find as you look back upon your life that the moments when you have really lived are the moments when you have done things in a spirit of love.

—Henry Drummond, 18th-century English poet

Emotional Power

From the position of the deep Self, the self that gives you life and inspiration, you are in charge of what emotions you generate. We have the ability to choose which emotions we have humming through us as we drive down the street, or greet the children, or answer the phone, or kiss our partners. You can run your typical emotional responses, or you can choose again. Choosing again in the midst of a habit is a powerful shift, and very satisfying.

One night a lover told me that he was ending our relationship and moving 3,000 miles away. I was stunned by his announcement, even though I knew he'd been stirring something around in his mind and was expecting any number of declarations from him. I had been working on the computer when he came in to talk with me, and my response to his statement was very much in that mode. Closing my eyes, I saw a pull-down menu of possible emotional responses. I mentally clicked on the menu and saw: get pissed, be in peace, be hurt, be relieved, or fall apart. I laughed. It was clear that his decision had very little to do with my experience; I simply had to choose what mood I wanted to engage.

Realizing that you are the one choosing to feel or not is very empowering. Practicing it is a little slippery at first. Emotions arrive quickly on the scene because we've already preprogrammed some responses: to coo and giggle at puppies, to rage at injustice, to get defensive when someone doesn't respond to us the way we want them to.

To regain the power of our emotions, we need to practice with little things first. For instance, find the emotional tone you'd like to have in your voice when you answer the phone at work. Is it impatience? Curiosity? Annoyance? Enthusiasm? Unconditional positive regard? Choose one and place a note by the phone with your word on it. Before answering the phone, take a few seconds to feel the quality of emotion you'd like to offer the caller. Watch what kind of experience you generate in that conversation with your tone in place; it's fascinating. We can cultivate the emotional tone we'd like to experience as an undercurrent to all the whimsies bouncing around on the surface of life. Choosing emotional tones that ground us in our hearts, in realms of acceptance and appreciation, gives us a deep sense of regeneration, nourishment, and abundance.

Practicing Emotional Choice

This is a meditation practice that nurtures our ability to experience the fullness of emotion, at will. You may repeat this meditation using the same emotion for several sessions, or you may wish to try out a new one. It took me quite some time to cultivate an experience of patience, but the results were certainly worth the effort. We need a full range of emotional choices in order to move out of our habituated emotional positions. Which ones would you like to cultivate in the garden of your heart?

1. Sit in a comfortable position, with your spine straight, where you will not be disturbed for fifteen minutes.

2. Choose an emotion that you would like to cultivate. Let's say you choose joy, for example.

3. Allow yourself to really feel the energy of joy for a moment. Let it permeate your entire body and as much of the space in the room as you can manage. This feeling is your central focus point and what is going to be cultivated throughout the meditation.

4. From this feeling of joy, notice that there are sensations connected with the feeling of joy, like expansiveness. These secondary feelings are like rays coming from the central focus of joy.

5. Take that connected secondary feeling and wear it in your body now. Feel expansiveness.

6. Now go back to the central focus of joy, and include the fullness of expansiveness into your experience of joy.

7. After sitting with this expanded sense of joy, find another emotional quality that is a part of joy, like brilliance.

8. Feel brilliance for a while, then add it back to joy.

9. Once again, sit with your growing complexity of joy.

10. Repeat this process until you've added a half-dozen nuances to your original experience of joy.

11. When you've finished, notice everything about how you feel. And in your daily life, notice how much easier it is to tap into joy.

The Yummy Heart Meditation

This is a practice of gratitude and celebration that aligns your energy fields with that which you would like to receive in your life. What we focus upon and vibrate in harmony with is what we manifest in our life. Appreciation is the direct path to creating more of what we want in our life.

In some cultures it is taught that the subtle sound that emanates from the heart center is *yummm,* and that this same chakra (see Lesson 4) is the point of receivership in our energy system. In this practice we enhance the energetic resonance of the heart by chanting its sound, and align our manifestation process by intentionally acknowledging that which we appreciate.

1. Sit or lie in a comfortable place, feet on the floor and spine straight.

2. Grounding is essential for bringing your dreams down to earth. Take a couple of diaphragmatic breaths and ground yourself, using the Kegel/heart breath exercise from Lesson 4, or by imagining yourself growing roots from your feet into the earth, or through whatever grounding practice you enjoy.

3. Continue deep breathing. On the exhalation, say "Yummm, yummm, yummm," until you run out of breath. Practice this for several breaths until it feels easy. If you can cultivate harmonic overtones when you chant, go ahead and do that. Play with your voice and the sound coming from deep in your body.

4. Keep the toning going, and allow a vision of someone or something that you desire or appreciate to come clearly to mind.

5. Each time you chant "yummm," open your heart and feel yourself receiving the desire or appreciation or celebration you're envisioning. Invite it in with a "yummm" sound.

6. Allow yourself to continue until your heart feels open, full, and ready to receive more of that which your heart desires and appreciates.

That farewell kiss which resembles greeting, that last glance of love
which becomes the sharpest pang of sorrow.

—*George Eliot, 19th-century English writer*

Endings

Through my work with bereavement clients, I've discovered that when someone leaves you, it matters greatly whether you feel them fully in your heart, or if you feel a sense of *not* having fully met each other the last times you were together. If it's the latter, you'll be left feeling an emptiness in your heart, a sense of unfinishedness that can last for a very long time. However, if you truly offered each other a little bit of your souls and hearts and bodies in that last good-bye kiss, the presence of that connection remains warm and present within you. The missing person feels close. These are the people who will tell you that "love never dies."

The man for whom I originally created Kissing School became a luscious kisser and then, about six months after we began his lessons, he died suddenly. I've always been grateful that we had learned to cultivate our loving. I felt blessed by the legacy, the clear truth that this moment is all we have to give. Why would I ever want to share less than the *kiss sublime*?

The truth is that we never know when our beloveds will be no longer with us. That is when all those small misses, the 10,000 distractions, the pecks on the fly become so much life lost, so much life that's empty of deep heart. Tomorrow there may be no more chances to share their heart, inhale their fragrance, partake of their mouth, have a conversation of souls. We have Now.

Share your self, your love, your private world again and again without postponing anything for later. Kiss your partner as if this were your last kiss, as if you were never going to see each other again. Don't waste this opportunity by slipping into a morbid state of mind, for this is your opportunity to celebrate love in the Now of this precious moment, a moment that may never return. Don't hold back. Give it your all!

EPILOGUE

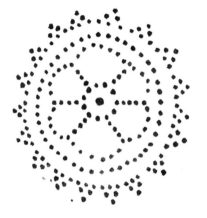

One kind kiss before we part,

Drop a tear and bid adieu;

Though we sever, my fond heart

Till we meet shall pant for you.

—*Robert Dodsley, 18th-century English writer*

Commence Adding Love to Your Life

Huzzah! You've made it all the way through the seven lessons of Kissing School, and congratulations are in order. It doesn't matter whether you skimmed or studied, whether you practiced the exercises or didn't even read them. What counts is that you have spent several hours reading about the possibility and practices for cultivating the arts of sublime loving and the sharing of rich intimacy. This simple act of reading changes the world in miraculous ways because, you see, we are all energetically woven together. When one person opens their heart, even for a moment, it becomes much more possible for the people around them, and the web of humanity as a whole, to open their hearts.

Moving toward our desires, fulfilling our dreams, enriching the quality of our loving are the big wins in life, because these acts of enrichment affect all the life around us. Each time your Inner Lover comes forward into your life, you become more soulfully empowered and capable of loving and being loved. In any moment of communion the illusion of separation vanishes for the moment, leaving instead a direct rapport with realm upon realm of love and life force. Heart and spirit emerge. Even if only for a few seconds, the veils of denial are thinned and an expansive, deep, harmonic, and vibrant experience of Oneness arrives. Every kiss that is now more heartful than a peck, every marginal hug that has shifted into a rich embrace, now feeds you and the hungry hearts of the world.

If you've been doing your Kissing School exercises, you're apt to be more relaxed, more fully present in your body, and more grounded to the earth than when you began. The instrument of your body-mind is tuned in, ready to turn on. You're Here, Now, with a charged energy system, an expanded bliss tolerance, and a willingness to luxuriate in your loving. There is more sharing of emotions and a greater ease of communication, both verbal and lip-laced. You're bound to have a more conscious, trusting connection to your inner self, allowing you to open beyond the box of habit and mediocrity into the sublime. Your simple act of contemplating a deeper intimacy plucks the energy strings of the holographic web and plays a love song. You're ready to dance in the rhythms of breath, heart, lip, and caress.

Stabilizing Love

Be mindful, dear student, that your old habits have inertia, a tendency to pull you back toward your previous norm. Every new loving experience you cultivate needs to be consciously recognized, celebrated, and revivified many times so that it becomes the new norm. Talk about these new changes with your beloved, your family, your friends. Journal about them, dream up new practices, and expand your repertoire. Keep the process alive until you develop a new inertial direction toward luscious loving, deeply given.

I will leave you with one new exercise for stabilizing your experience of living an intimate life, an exercise to strengthen and support your new loving habits. I also invite you and your beloved to attend my Kissing School playshop (it's really not a "work" shop) and share several hours of lips-on practice. Here the two of you can surrender into the moment and be guided into deep, rich, luscious lip play. Many of my students have asked if they can come to Kissing School more than once. Oh, definitely! Some wise lovers have come three times and found that they learn more and more each time.

If, after graduating from the Kissing School playshop, you find that you like the experience of being an empowered lover and having your energy ignited, then you may be ready for my graduate course in intimacy: *Spirit in the Flesh*. This energy embodiment training comprises the essential, core teachings of the traditional sexual mastery schools, and cultivates your ability to access and circulate the energy and potency of your deepest Self. The training offers your Inner Lover the energy mastery skills necessary to explore the practices and techniques of deep sexual communion that are taught in my *Spirit of Sex* course. This is a class for integrating the tantric energy embodiment practices you learned in *Spirit in the Flesh* into deep advanced sexual intimacy techniques. The energy practices add the fire and intensity of deep intimacy into every touch—igniting your heart, spirit, and sexual charge.

If you've been practicing your Kissing School lessons, you may have awoken to insights and skills that have deepened your experience of kissing and intimacy. I'd love to hear your stories—feel free to write me. Information on all the above classes and playshops can be found at www.KissingSchool.com.

Congratulations once again, bodacious lovers, and thank you for your courage, your passion, and your desire to kiss and love deeply. Go forth, and commence sharing your juiciest *kiss sublime*!

Graduation Exercise: Putting Love on the List

I was sitting outside the market one day, quickly trying to remember the items on the grocery list that I'd left at home. I closed my eyes and waited for my mind to focus and gather the information. The message that came to mind rushed through my body, leaving shivers and goose bumps. It said, "Put love on the list."

"Oh yeah, I'll pick some up," I thought. "I think I saw it on the bread aisle."

I closed my eyes again. The message repeated, only louder: **"Put love on the list!"**

Well, that got my attention, but it took another few moments until I understood what was being asked of me. It was as if all the ingredients for a rich and luscious love life were to be collected along with the Swiss chard and the yogurt. I was instructed to write down my groceries, and every second or third item was to be a *quality of loving* that I'd like to have more of. I was going to the market for love and dinner. Swiss chard, apples, and appreciation. I was not to leave the fruit stand until I allowed myself to experience a full measure of appreciation, right then—for any ol' thing!

OK, that felt good. Now: honey, almond butter, and joy. "*Feeeeel* the joy coursing through your body. See how it lightens your load, Cherie?" Oh yeah!

I gathered up milk and sensual breathing; salmon, mustard, and the feeling of snuggling; tea, cat food, and the sense of lingering kisses all over my body.

Who knew grocery shopping could be so yummy?

Long before I reached the surprised cashier, I was radiant and grinning all over my body. That feeling lasted for hours, and I'm sure the food was imbued with magical powers by then.

I found out later that I could add love to all my lists: the to-do lists, phone call lists, lists of household repairs. It's a sneaky, fun, and profound way to cultivate the experience of loving, every day, any ol' where.

Notes

Notes

Notes

Notes

Notes

Notes

About the Author

Cherie Byrd, M.A., is a pioneer in the field of Energy Psychology and specializes in body/mind integration, sacred sexuality, and spiritual emergence. She has a private practice in Seattle and teaches internationally, integrating ancient healing practices with modern consciousness and energy-field research. She lives on a small island in Puget Sound, where she is known as an artist, mystic, and healer. For more information on Cherie and Kissing School! go to www.kissingschool.com.